0000210100

KT-486-279

371.9. (OHA)

Special Education Integration in Europe

Special Education Integration in Europe

Christine O'Hanlon

David Fulton Publishers
London

David Fulton Publishers Ltd
2 Barbon Close, London WC1N 3JX

First published in Great Britain by
David Fulton Publishers 1993

Note: The right of the author to be identified as the author of this work has been asserted
by her in accordance with the Copyright, Designs and Patents Act 1988.

Copyright © Christine O'Hanlon

British Library Cataloguing in Publication Data

A catalogue record for this book is available from the British Library

ISBN 1-85346-236-5

All rights reserved. No part of this publication may be reproduced, stored in a retrieval
system or transmitted, in any form, or by any means, electronic, mechanical,
photocopying, recording or otherwise, without the permission of the publishers.

Typeset by ROM-Data Corporation Limited, Falmouth, Cornwall, England
Printed in Great Britain by BPCC Wheatons Ltd., Exeter

Contents

Acknowledgements

I am grateful to my sources in the different EC countries for their permission to reproduce amended versions of their original texts, to the Ministries of Education in each country, and in particular to EURYDICE without whose information I could not have proceeded. A special acknowledgement also goes to J. Hansen, C. Pastor and Maria Teresa Fernandes, whose writing has provided useful source material for this book. Thanks are also due to my friends in ATEE Working Group 7 whose collaboration together since the early 1980s has given me the insight and motivation to write about integration in Europe. Finally I would like to acknowledge the contribution of a number of people who lent their support in the typing and translation of documents. They are Judy Dandy, Savita Anderson and Catherine O'Hanlon, without whose help the book would not have been written.

Introduction

The European Community

Any political system must respond to the needs of its people and the European Community is no exception. The Community aims to do this in two ways. First, all forms of economic integration are also aimed towards social progress. The basic freedoms of the Common Market cover not just the economic objective of a large internal market but also the individual freedoms which guarantee Community citizens a minimum measure of personal self-realization which transcends national frontiers.

Second, the door to significant progress in policy areas which directly affect the social life and well-being of all Europeans was opened at the Paris Summit in 1972, when the Heads of State or governments agreed on the need for a common approach to social and regional policy which includes education. It is clear that education is to play an increasing role in the 'new Europe' (Preston, 1991).

The European Community is an international organization which links 12 countries wishing to work together. It consists of 12 member states and 325 million citizens. The six founding countries – France, Belgium, the Federal Republic of Germany, Italy, Luxembourg and the Netherlands – were joined by Denmark, Ireland and the United Kingdom in 1973, by Greece in 1981 and by Spain and Portugal in 1986. The Single European Act of 1986 spells out the objectives of the Community which is generally, the completion of the European internal market and the creation by 1992 of a great area without frontiers. This aim includes technological development, economic and monetary union, social cohesion, and the improvement of the environment and the working environment. The Act also aims to make the

Community work more effectively and more democratically.

The Community traces its origins to the Treaty of Paris in 1951, and then signing of the two Treaties of Rome in 1957 which marked the setting up of the European Economic Community (EEC). The single European Act of 1986 amends and complements these Treaties, spelling out the aims of what is now known as the European Community (EC). The major changes introduced in 1987 by the Single European Act included giving the Community wider powers in the social field to enable it to press ahead with the coherent European social policy on which it had already embarked. The social dimension has become a vital part of the single market project, to make fuller and more effective use of resources and to distribute the benefits more fairly; this includes education.

Social policy accounts for 7 per cent of the total spending in the European Community budget. Most of this money is spent through the European Social Fund which co-finances training and re-training schemes and aid for recruitment. There is a focus on young people and on the long-term unemployed, especially in regions affected by industrial decline or lack of development. In addition, there is an increased allocation for young people, particularly within exchange programmes such as Erasmus, Comett, and 'Youth for Europe'. In this way the Community aims to make a social network in the large market of 1992 (EC, 1989).

Social policy which finances a social action programme comprises some 40 measures aimed at full and better employment, improved living and working conditions and increased involvement of member countries in social partnership. The Commission has proposed underpinning the foundations of Community social policy by means of a Social Charter of basic rights which will reflect the European model of society, social dialogue, and the rights of each individual in the Community (EC, 1990). In 1989 the 'Community Charter of Fundamental Social Rights' when adopted by the Council became the 'Community Charter of Fundamental Social Rights for workers' (from which the UK abstained). A more wide reaching European Social Charter to include all citizens is still anticipated, and it is hoped will include specific political issues related to the lives of people with disabilities and special needs (Daunt 1991).

Community operation

The Community operates with wide powers to formulate, shape and implement a Community policy. The Council of Ministers stands at centre stage and consists of ministers from Member State governments and makes the major policy decisions of the Community. It is the Council, acting on a proposal from the Commission which takes the decisions necessary for the attainment of the goals laid down in the Treaties. Ensuring freedom of movement, freedom to provide services and the right of establishment, defining common policies, and establishing the Community budget are some of its responsibilities.

The Commission is the engine of Community policy, the guardian of the Treaties and the advocate of the Community interest. It is made up of 17 members who are required to act in complete independence for the good of the Community. The Commission is responsible for making proposals for Community measures to the Council; without such proposals the Council cannot, as a rule, take any action. The Commission is responsible to the European Parliament. The Commission must defend and justify its position in public debates before Parliament in full session and present an annual general report on the activities of the Communities for discussion. Parliament may deliver opinions on Commission proposals before the Council takes a decision.

The inter-institutional cooperation procedure adopted by the EC related to major decisions basically follows the route of:

1. *Commission* makes a proposal.
2. *Parliament* at first reading of the proposal adopts a 'common position' (which is its version of a Commission proposal).
3. The *Council* passes the legislation set out in the 'common position'.
4. *Parliament* receives proposals for a second reading – may amend or reject the document through an absolute majority.
5. *Commission* receives documents and decides whether to accept or reject.
6. *Council* receives documents in either case and the legislation is passed by a qualified majority or by a unanimous vote.

Before a Commission proposal can be adopted by the Council, an opinion must be sought, not only from the European Parliament, but also, in many cases, from the Community's Economic and Social Committee. This is a consultative committee with 189 members who represent employers, trade unions, consumers and other interested groups.

Community expenditure

The five major countries of the EC are Germany, France, the UK, Italy and Spain. These countries are by far the largest in terms of Gross Domestic Product (GDP), area and population in the EC. The GDP is the sum of final expenditure on goods and services, less the cost of imports.

One of the indicators often used to demonstrate the efforts being made by countries in the EC in the field of education is the percentage of their GDP that they devote to it. The GDP is influenced by several factors: the country's demographic structure, the distribution of school-age population at different levels of education, the volume of public expenditure as a whole, priorities within the budget, etc. Furthermore, the same percentage figure will not have the same significance in the case of a 'rich' country with a high per capita GDP as in the case of a 'poor' country where this figure is much lower.

The share of public expenditure of GDP in 1986 ranged between 5 and 6.5 per cent in 9 out of 22 countries surveyed by the OECD (OECD, 1990). The expenditure was very low in Greece (2.7 per cent) and relatively low in Germany and Portugal. By contrast, the figure exceeded 6.5 per cent in the Netherlands, Luxembourg and Denmark.

In the same report, figures related to the total public expenditure on education in 1987 as a percentage of total public expenditure in each country, shows Denmark and the UK at the top, with 13.2 per cent and 11.5 per cent respectively, whereas the lowest percentages were Luxembourg and Spain with 6.5 per cent and 6.0 per cent respectively. So it is difficult to make definitive judgements or hold a theory related to expenditure in relation to GDP in member countries because of alternative rises and falls in the figures published in relation to expenditure and its relationship to GDP over the last decade or more. However, the five major countries in the EC accounted in 1990 for 87 per cent of the total community GDP and for 84 per cent of its population (Somers, 1991).

The EC's commitment to integration

In confirmation of the EC's committment to 'integration', in 1987 the Council passed the following proposals concerning a programme of European collaboration on the integration of 'handicapped' children (as they are predominantly referred to in European documentation) into ordinary schools to :

- reaffirm the importance of achieving the maximum possible integration of handicapped children into ordinary schools, as well as the main measures mentioned in those conclusions concerning elimination of physical obstacles, training of teachers, development of school curricula and gaining understanding among families and the local community;
- emphasize the need to continue working on the conclusions in the context of the Community programme for the general social integration of handicapped people;
- agree that future work at the levels of the member states and the European

Community should also take into account considerations concerning future work on the integration of handicapped children into ordinary schools.

In 1990 the Council continued their proposals on the basis that they were convinced that the education policy of all the member states was evolving towards integration – for children and young people with disabilities into ordinary systems of education, with the support as appropriate of the specialized sector and/or services in varying degrees according to each state. They proceeded to adopt resolutions to:

1. Agree to intensify, where necessary, their efforts to integrate or encourage integration of pupils and students with disabilities, in all appropriate cases, into the ordinary education system.
2. Consider full integration into the system of mainstream education as a first option in all appropriate cases.
3. See the work of special schools and centres for children and young people with disabilities as complementary to the work of the ordinary education systems.
4. Develop the skills and teaching methods used in special education for the disposal of mainstream education for the benefit of the children and young people with special needs who are educated there.
5. Promote the integration of children and young people with disabilities into the various sectors of mainstream education and so contribute to their acquiring autonomy and independence.
6. Increase the use of the educational potential of new technology to aid communication and the development of language skills.
7. (i) Facilitate the integration of children and young people with disabilities into mainstream education, with particular reference to the following areas:

   – the initial and in-service training of teachers in the area of special needs,
   – the participation of families and social and community agencies,
   – the allocation of available resources for education,
   – the most comprehensive possible support for the global needs of the child and adolescent by the implementation of an individual developmental, pedagogical, social and therapeutic plan,
   – the creation of new resources,
   – the availability of and access to suitable assessment services,
   – the introduction of curricular innovations,
   – the adaptation of existing regulations and the organization of education so as to do away with structural barriers to integration;

(ii) develop the role played by specialized institutions and their teachers in promoting the development of integrated education, for example:

- by utilizing them, where they exist, as centres and resource teams for ongoing training of teachers who need more information on disability and special educational needs,
- by recruiting from them, where appropriate, peripatetic teachers to support children with disabilities in ordinary classes,
- by increasing cooperation between mainstream schools and specialized institutions in developing special teaching programmes,
- by developing individualized programmes and teaching methods and, where necessary, other educational strategies which meet the needs of the children and young people;

(iii) develop active cooperation between the education services and other services such as health services, social services, etc. in preparing, promoting and ensuring continuity and consistency in the integration programmes;

(iv) encourage the formulation of comprehensive and coherent policies, with regard especially to the organization of educational provision, the supply and management of resources, the monitoring and evaluation of integration schemes and the dissemination of good practices;

(v) overcome difficulties which curricula in mainstream education may present for children and young people with disabilities by developing individualized learning programmes and by promoting the use of new technology as an additional means of stimulating communication and learning in schools.

The final resolution was to ensure that all the activities and programmes which were supported in the areas of education, training and youth policy and transition to adult and working life generally take account of the special needs of people with disabilities who wish to participate in them.

What is integration?

Since the publication of the Warnock Report in 1978 there has been a central policy thrust in the UK and throughout Europe for the integration of children with special educational needs (SENs) into ordinary schools. The concept of integration has been in currency in Europe for many years. In the UK, in 1976, the Snowdon Working Party referred to integration as 'the absence of segregation... as social acceptance'. An OECD report (1981) defined integration as 'providing handicapped children with an education which meets their special needs in ordinary rather than special schools'. Booth

(1983) describes integration as 'the process of increasing the participation of children and young people in their communities'. There are differing conceptual bases for integration that have been well elaborated by writers in the UK, the USA and Europe (eg, Booth, 1991; Booth and Potts, 1983; Cope and Anderson, 1977; Cuomo, 1991; Fish, 1991; Hegarty, 1991; Kirk and Gallagher, 1979; Soder, 1991). Successful practice has been reported in the UK and in Europe (eg, Ainscow and Tweddle, 1992; Bennett and Cass, 1989; Booth and Swann, 1987; Bovair *et al.*, 1992; Galloway and Goodwin, 1979; Hegarty *et al.*, 1981; Hodgson *et al.*, 1984; Lewis, 1990; Lindsay and Clough, 1991; Madden and Slavin, 1983; Swann, 1981). There is a well-established common commitment to the principle of integration, or the inclusion of children in ordinary schools in the extensive literature on the subject.

Recent research has also shown that children's needs can be met in the mainstream, so that the categorization of pupils which defined their special schooling in the past is no longer appropriate. Research studies show that:

• growing numbers of parents and children are requesting integrated rather than segregated educational placements;
• more professionals are enthusiastic to adapt old ways of working to face the new challenges of whole-school policies and curricula for all;
• that education authorities have shown themselves to be responsive and flexible to change; recent evidence in the UK shows that a majority of local education authorities are now placing more children with disabilities or difficulties in learning, in mainstream schools rather than special schools.

This has come about by the changing of attitudes; the re-allocation of resources and the expertise from special schools; the development of in-sevice training for those in special and ordinary schools; the reduction of the proportion of children selected for separate special school education; and the committment to putting the integration principle into action (Swann, 1991).

It is now possible to find evidence and to see in practice diverse ordinary contexts where all children can be included. The subject of integration is no longer debated. It is the best interests of the child which are put first in making decisions about the best quality of education for that child. There is a move towards the monitoring of the quality of the integration experience and its advantages for education systems and the pupils who are the recipients of the new educational experiences.

Yet there are still difficulties expressed through the use of the term 'integration' itself as witnessed by Booth (1991), Soder (1991) and Hegarty

(1991). Booth and Soder point out the significance of language and terminology in the attitudes we hold and the understanding we possess in the area
of special needs in education. Booth points out the cultural unacceptability
of the term 'normalization' in a UK context, and Soder refers to the
moralistic rather than scientific support for ideas like integration. In the UK
at present it appears that the word 'integration' is now being replaced by
terms such as 'inclusive education' or 'increased participation' in schooling,
which suggests a more positive and less emotive view of what is increasingly being emphasized as a 'process' and not a 'state'. 'Inclusive
education' is being used now to refer to forms of education that are
organized to include special needs provision; this phrase overcomes the
implication that 'integration' occurs after prior segregation.

Hegarty (1991) accepts that in Europe generally, the fundamentals of
integrated education are understood in principle. It is about new conceptions
of ordinary schooling, the reform of schools and fitting schools to pupils rather
than of developing individual pupil programmes, pupil placement and social-
izing pupils to 'norms' of learning and behaviour. In Europe or beyond he
asserts that the term 'integration' should be banned so that we can clarify the
different processes that are referred to in the complex variety of full- and
part-time placement for pupils with special needs in education. This is
because integration in different countries is based on different value positions.
These values reflect different priorities in education which range from basic
human rights to social participation or the quality of pedagogy in schools. This
leads to misunderstanding and claims from country to country about 'good'
practices which are not comparable to efforts towards integration in other
countries which also claim to aim for the 'best' education through the quality
of their practice and their aims for integration of pupils with special needs.
For this reason it is difficult too, for the researcher, to undertake comparative
studies from the data available in Europe because of different approaches,
practices and priorities, and not least because of differences in the form of
data collection undertaken in member states. Different sources consulted in
the research of this book have shown widely different estimates of pupils
receiving special schooling in the countries consulted; there is also a divergence of information about the same situation, which can cause confusion eg,
from OECD (1990), UNESCO (1988) and EC research studies (Pijl and
Meijer, 1991). These research studies collect similar information by asking
different research questions which leads to differential and often conflicting
data. The practice of indicating the category or type of 'handicap' that has
been identified within the child is not necessarily an indication of the need for
special school provision or for special resources in the ordinary school. The
special educational provision necessary for a percentage of school age

children should indicate more precisely the 'in' school response, rather than the 'in' child problem when one is identifying the necessary resources and support in a European context.

The different ideological positions taken by the definition of educational policies in EC countries reflect the differences in their cultures, traditions and social structure. In the 12 countries examined in this book there are differences in the number of years of compulsory schooling from a starting point of between 4–7 years, to a terminal point of between 14–16 years. In the legislative and policy-making practices there are differences in respect to formulating the law through general directives for ordinary schooling or in passing special laws for 'handicapped' pupils. There are different methods for deciding what constitutes a 'handicap' or a 'special need', there are differences in the general viewing of children as in need of special provision temporarily, or at some time in their school career, as against the rigid setting of categories and formulas which lead to specialized, permanent and separate forms of schooling. The result is a wide variation in the countries studied in the number of children identified as 'handicapped' and the subsequent variety or forms of special provision, from full or partial mainstream placement, to specialized placements in schools or hospitals made on medical rather than educational priorities. The development of research projects through the financial support of the EC has encouraged a greater awareness and understanding of some of the deep national and structural differences that exist, and has enabled debate and attitudinal change in national and international forums. After the United Nations declared 1981 to be the International Year of Disabled People, the first Action Programme to promote the social and economic integration of disabled people was established in 1982, closely followed in 1988 by the second action programme, HELIOS. In the early 1980s too, the Association of Teacher Education in Europe (ATEE) working group on the subject of special education was initiated and was subsequently developed by a core of stable members who engaged in educational debate through a series of symposia and conferences in Amsterdam, Koln, Belfast, London, Barcelona, Lisbon, Utrecht and Dublin (Diniz, 1991) which were heavily subsidized by the EC Bureau in favour of Action for the Disabled. In the late 1980s a series of educational networks has been established through the RIF (Reseau d'Institutions de Formation) under the auspices of the European Community Youth Exchange Bureau, including one which is entitled 'The European Dimension in Education, and the Education of Handicapped Children in School'. Membership of both has enabled me to develop and extend my understanding of special needs in education in a Europe-wide context and to prompt the writing of this book.

CHAPTER 1

Belgium

Belgium is a small country in the North West of Europe with a population of approximately 10 million. The official languages are Flemish and French. In the Kingdom of Belgium there are parallel systems of education, ordinary schools and special schools. Special education exists to cater for the educational needs of children and adolescents who can benefit from education but who are nevertheless unable to benefit from the ordinary school.

Admission to a special school is subject to multidisciplinary examinations carried out by approved psycho-medico-social centres and decided according to the pupils' needs and pedagogical capabilities. The law dated 6 July 1986 has established integrated education for certain types of handicapped pupils. Special education is organized according to the physical, sensory, psychological or intellectual handicaps of the pupils, and its main aim is to integrate handicapped children as much as possible, first into a school environment, then into society. The basis for the organization of this type of education was laid down in the law dated 6 July 1970. Certain schools had already been giving such education for many years, but in the absence of proper controls.

Special education is organized at three levels: nursery, primary and secondary. Handicapped children may be enrolled in nursery schools at 3 years of age, and may continue at that level until the age of 8 years if they derive any benefit from their attendance. Special educational facilities are provided for all categories of handicapped children, except for those suffering from speech disorders or moderate and serious learning difficulties.

Entry to special primary school is between 6 and 8 years of age, and the pupil normally leaves at the age of 13, 14 or 15. Studies at secondary level may be continued up to the age of 22, but pupils may be granted exemptions from the age conditions.

Particular enrolment conditions

Apart from the age conditions, enrolment in special educational establishments is subject to a procedure involving the preparation of a very thorough report, including a certificate and a record of supporting observations. The report must conclude that the pupil has a real need to attend a special school. It must also define the type of schooling best suited to the nature and seriousness of the handicap, the level of education and the most suitable school.

Eight forms of special education have been created in order to provide facilities in accordance with the pupils' needs. They are as follows:

1. For children and adolescents with slight mental retardation (not at nursery school level).
2. For children and adolescents with moderate and/or severe mental retardation.
3. For children and adolescents with emotional disturbances.
4. For children and adolescents with physical deficiencies.
5. For children and adolescents with learning difficulties.
6. For children and adolescents with visual deficiencies.
7. For children and adolescents with auditory deficiencies.
8. For children and adolescents with disorders of speech or language and/or serious learning difficulties (not provided at nursery and secondary levels).

In view of the complexity and difficulty of the pupils' problems, the teachers may be assisted by psychological, medical and paramedical staff, such as speech therapists, physiotherapists, paediatric nurses, etc., for specific remedial treatment. In exceptional cases, the child may receive instruction at home.

Four forms of education are organized at the level of special secondary education. The courses are usually organized in common for several types of special education in each form. The enrolment report which directs a pupil towards special secondary education must mention not only the type of special education but also the appropriate form and content.

If it is considered advisable to transfer a pupil from one form of education to another during a given school year, the Class Board and the steering body are requested to make their recommendations. The parents are, of course, involved in the decision. At least once a year the team makes an assessment of the integrated education plan, and is obliged to inform the parents of its conclusions. The schools receive an annual subsidy based on the integration per pupil within the integrated education plan, which enables them to fund special provision and support.

Integration of Disabled Pupils in the Regular School System in the Dutch-speaking Community of Belgium

August Dens

The legal framework and related developments (1970–86)

The Special Education Act (1970)

Developments in the integration of the disabled in education have resulted from the Special Education Act, which was unanimously adopted by Parliament in 1970. The main integration-orientated principles clearly stated in the Act were that:

1. The implementation of the Act's provisions was limited to the genuinely *handicapped*, and special education was to be provided only when really needed and then only as long as necessary.
2. Parallel to the development of special education, preventative action was to be undertaken in ordinary education mostly through remedial education and differentiated opportunities offered in elementary and vocational education.
3. Each *handicap* was to be defined on an educational basis, so that educational needs and potential of the pupil were to determine his or her ultimate referral to a special school.
4. Special education was to be regarded as a right, never an obligation and parents would have the final say where the referral procedures were concerned.
5. Social integration was to be the specific aim pursued in all forms of special education.

Regulations for the Organisation of Special Education (1978)

1. Admittance to special education was to be governed by strict regulations implemented by independent boards and persons outside schools. This was designed to uphold the principle that says that no pupil should be referred to special education when an ordinary school can offer sufficient opportunities for education.
2. Three out of every four potential special education pupils could not be admitted to a special school before they were 6 years old. Special

education would not be provided at pre-school level to cater for children with mild mental disabilities, nor for those with specific learning difficulties. All these children would start their education in an ordinary school until it became apparent that they could no longer cope.

3. For one out of four pupils in primary special schools there would be no corresponding upper secondary provision. Therefore, pupils with learning difficulties who were educated in primary special schools were expected to be integrated into ordinary education, at age 13 at the latest. Only in exceptional circumstances would these pupils be allowed to attend the special school for another year, or even two.

4. The different forms of curricular provision in secondary special education were aimed to maximize integration. Vocational special education was designed to provide the necessary preparation for integration into an ordinary living and working environment; three quarters of the total number of secondary special education units would provide this form of vocational preparation.

5. Young people with sensory and motor impairment who are of normal intellectual ability would be offered training similar to that in ordinary schools; the scheme would award diplomas of equal merit and therefore offer the same opportunities for 'transition'.

Continuous guidance: PMS centres [1]

During their years of attending a special school all pupils would be under the continuous supervision of an external specialist centre (PMS) which would be responsible for guidance and cooperate with the internal educational team in school. These centres were meant to ensure objectivity whenever decisions as to whether a pupil should remain in special education or be transferred to ordinary education were taken. Should a controversy arise, the advice of a consultative committee would be sought. The aforesaid committee would then decide by arbitration (Min Ond, 1988, pp. 46–8).

Innovation in the provision of integrated education (1980–86)

The experiment in integrated education (1980–83)

In March 1980 special teams were assigned to five special education establishments or their guidance services. These teams were set up specifically to help pupils with motor disabilities or visually and hearing impaired pupils who attended classes in ordinary schools. The pupils had returned to regular education after attending special schools or had, despite the severity of their disabilities, chosen to stay in their ordinary school.

The project mainly served the purpose of undertaking an assessment of the conditions determining a pupil's chances of being successfully integrated in ordinary education. The criteria used concerned the nature of the disability, the individual characteristics of the pupils, his or her social environment, parents, teaching staff, fellow pupils and the school in its entirety. From the results of the enquiry, recommendations for general implementation of integrated education were proposed.

Generalized implementation (September 1983): main features

In September 1983, integrated education was extended to include all pupils with motor, visual and hearing impairment. As such, this was seen as a form of special education operating outside special schools. The main characteristic of integrated education was cooperation between the mainstream school and its special counterpart where teachers and members of the paramedical staff (speech therapists and physiotherapists) provided extra help to pupils with special needs who were attending an ordinary school on a full-time basis; in addition, they assisted the teaching staff and helped with curriculum development and delivery.

Integrated education was intended for pupils who, on account of their disability, were entitled to special education but would and could make use of their right to education in an ordinary school.

Responsibility for the assessment of their special needs remained with the same guidance services and persons as those responsible for referral to special education. These teams employed a multidisciplinary approach and observation data provided by schools and parents were taken into account. The decision regarding the admission of a child to integrated education was linked to a concrete plan of special action. This *Integration Plan* became the indispensable basis for the implementation of integrated education. Consultation and cooperation by all concerned, including the parents, was strongly emphasized. The implementation of the *Integration Plan* was the responsibility of the two schools that undertook to cooperate, directly involving the guidance centres and the parents. Together they determined the real dimension of the pupils' need for help and drew attention to the special assistance which should be provided.

The special school where special assistance was given was allowed extra hours on the timetable and extra funds to cover operational costs. For each pupil in integrated education a weekly credit of two hours educational help or physiotherapy was allowed. For the visually impaired who use Braille, schools received four extra hours. Grants were paid principally to cover the cost of ambulatory guidance. In principle, every special school could give the support provided in the *Integration Plan*.

The *Integration Plan* and its implementation were subject to yearly assessment by those parties who contributed to its implementation. In so doing, the pupils' development and the changing circumstances in the school where the child attends the classes were taken into account.

New legislation (1986)

The Special and Integrated Education Act (11 March 1986)

This new Act modified the 1970 Act and mirrors changes of attitude towards the education and care of the disabled. The Act's objectives are:

1. The right to special education has now been phrased in a positive way. The uncompromising and negative provision whereby attending an ordinary school was *impossible*, has now been repealed. According to the new Act, a pupil is only required to attend special education in so far as his or her educational needs and potential become apparent during a multidisciplinary assessment. What is more, a legal contract is being devised so as to provide extra specialist support for disabled pupils attending ordinary classes.
2. The explanatory statement accompanying the Act stresses the importance of special and integrated education. That special education has a right to exist and that it serves its purpose is acknowledged. For some pupils it still remains the best opportunity for social integration. However, for other disabled children and in certain circumstances, integrated education in the mainstream may offer the best opportunities, provided special educational support is forthcoming.
3. The choice between special education and regular education is to be made after consultation with all those involved, ie, the parents, the schools and their guidance centres.
4. Integrated education does not constitute a novelty; it is not a third kind of education halfway between regular education and special education. Accordingly, the range of application of the 1970 Act has not been changed, as integrated education remains a form of special education. It ensures that special education is available to special needs pupils in regular classes. By their cooperation, the regular and special education sectors have narrowed the gap which for a number of years had separated the two systems and which had perceptibly widened.

5. In the new Act the remedial and integrating task of the (entire) special education system has been stressed and promoted. Thus the first move is made towards a less area-bound definition of special education and a more quality-conscious approach to education in general.

Furthermore, it is made clear that specialist training and continuing education for teachers are essential requirements in special education. Teachers in regular schools would need special support in order to cope with the special needs of pupils in their classes. Teachers in special education on the other hand, should get extra training in order to develop competence to provide support, consultancy and training to colleagues in regular schools.

Establishing the statutory requirements

In pursuance of the 1986 Act, the Central Advisory Board for Special Education advised on the rules and regulations which are to be applied to Integrated Education. The first draft of a royal decree is being discussed with a view to defining the means and the criteria for obtaining additional staff. The organizational details are to be set out by ministerial order, so that the varying experience and the different insights acquired in the field of integrated education in both areas of the country may be taken into account. In the course of the discussions the following factors of the mainstreaming policy have been outlined:

- Integration may be encouraged from within the existing special education system, for instance by breaking though the *barriers* separating the different types, levels and forms of provision. This new trend reflects changes in thinking about existing classifications of special needs and types of provision.
- As far as school organization is concerned, the pupils should be grouped according to the similarity of their educational needs and potential. In each individual case the pupils are to be assessed on a multidisciplinary basis. The physical, psychological and social characteristics of each pupil provide important data, but on their own they are of little value in decisions about appropriate curriculum and pedagogy, and even less so for classification in educational categories.
- Special education establishments would now be able to provide more external integration of special needs children, namely by organizing activities jointly with the ordinary schools. Of course, the initiative would have to come from special education.
- Different mainstreaming formulae would be possible. Up to now there

has been a tendency to consider the complete and permanent integration of special needs pupils, which mean strict requirements have to be met. In different circumstances, partial and temporary integration might prove possible for yet more pupils.

- The general procedures for referral to integrated education have been maintained. They specifically concern pupils: (i) who are entitled to receive special education; (ii) who also fulfil the conditions of admission to integrated education; and (iii) for whom regular class placement has been explicitly laid down in an Integration Plan, involving all those concerned.
- The existing integrated education system may be extended to all types of special needs. The requirements as well as the mode of implementation may vary accordingly. When the integrated pupil gets additional support from a special school, regularity, frequency and the presence of supportive services in the vicinity are very important factors.
- Sometimes, this is likely to cause problems when less frequent types of special education have to be organized by isolated specialist institutions. A solution will have to be found, so that the need for adequate support can be reconciled with the need for regularity and frequency and no precious time is lost on journeys between sites.
- The degree of the disability will no doubt be the main issue raised during the discussion. In that sense the admission policy and the criteria for referral will have to be defined. It is clear that the higher the degree of disability the more specialized (ie, categorical) provision will be needed. We should however beware of creating still more needs on the pretext of more specialized care in cases where the ordinary school – now as in the past – can provide a viable solution using its own resources.

Survey of participation rates in integrated education

Development of integrated education since 1983

Since September 1983 the number of special needs pupils in integrated education has more than doubled (see Table 1.1). The increase is perceptible chiefly at pre-school and at primary school levels. In fact, the number of pupils with motor disability and hearing impairment has tripled; those with visual impairment were strongly represented from the beginning and therefore their number has increased relatively slowly.

The ratio of integrated pupils (percentage of integrated pupils as compared with the total number of pupils attending special education of the same

Table 1.1 Integrated education: number of pupils (N) and per cent integration (%)

	1983–1984		1988–1989		1990–1991	
	N	%	N	%	N	%
Total	234	8.26	740	26.10	708	19.70
Pre-school + primary	129	8.65	536	33.23	521	24.61
Secondary	105	7.84	204	16.69	187	12.67
Motor handicap	41	2.56	256	15.39	244	12.38
Visual handicap	109	27.95	212	53.81	202	33.06
Auditory handicap	84	10.01	272	34.96	262	25.91

% = N (I.Ed.) x 100/N (S.Ed.)

type) has risen from 8 per cent (1983) to 26 per cent (1989). For the visually impaired, the percentage has risen to 54 per cent in 1989; for the motor disabled, it was just over 15 per cent and for the hearing impaired the integration ratio was almost 35 per cent.

However, in 1991 the percentages of pupils in these categories who are in integrated education has fallen slightly from 26 to 20 per cent overall. The largest group to be integrated are still pupils with visual impairment at 33 per cent, closely followed by hearing impaired pupils at 26 per cent, with motor impaired pupils following at 12 per cent integration.

Participation in mainstreaming has varied according to the area involved. In fact, there are three cluster areas covered by three large supporting establishments. Could it be that there is a case of supply being a contributory factor to demand? Apart from these cluster areas, mainstreaming is varied and has many ramifications. This situation invites questions as to whether consultation and cooperation between the different parties involved is a practicable proposition.

Where do pupils in integrated education come from?

Education previously received The original aim of increasing the numbers of special school pupils who are integrated into regular schools has only been upheld in 27.5 per cent of cases; 72.5 per cent of all integrated education pupils come from regular schools. Most direct admissions involve infant and primary school children (85 per cent) and the visually impaired (82 per cent). At the secondary school level, nearly equal numbers come from regular or special schools (see Table 1.2). This is mainly because a great many hearing impaired pupils have transferred from a primary special school to a regular secondary school.

20

Table 1.2 Former school attendance of integrated education pupils

	Regular school (%)	Special school (%)
Total	72.5	27.5
Pre-school + primary	84.8	15.1
Secondary	51.6	48.3
Motor handicap	77.5	22.4
Visual handicap	82.3	17.6
Auditory handicap	60.1	39.8

Social background Working-class children are two to three times less likely to receive integrated education than segregated special education (see Table 1.3). On the other hand, the attendance level of upper-middle-class children in integrated education is three to four times higher than in segregated special education. It cannot be denied that a social class factor is involved where access to integrated education is concerned. This factor is most strongly present in cases of hearing impaired and motor disabled children (Dens and Meskens, 1987).

How integrated education works and issues arising

A number of problems have come to light in a survey of 76 per cent of pupils receiving integrated education in grant-aided schools (80–85 per cent of all schools in Flanders are subsidized). Below we summarize its main findings (Dens *et al.*, 1986).

Table 1.3 Social background of special education and integrated education pupils

	Integrated education (%)	Special education–all (%)
Working class	33.3	66-90*
Employees	31.1	
Agricultural	3.2	
Independent/self-employed	10.7	
Upper class/management	19.3	5-7*
Others	2	

* Mean for different types of special education

Table 1.4 Prerequisites for fully integrated education

Conditions	Fulfilled	% of the number of pupils		
		More or less fulfilled	Almost not fulfilled	Not fulfilled
(1) Intelligence	63	23	10	1
(2) School level	47	27	17	3
(3) Motivation	73	17	5	1
(4) Ability to cope	60	31	5	-
(5) Family support	68	20	7	2
(6) Positive attitude to school	82	16	1	-
(7) Openness of classgroup	74	22	2	-

Requirements to be met by pupils in integrated education

At present, all the pupils receiving integrated education in Flanders have been fully integrated into the mainstream(see Table 1.4). This means that they have had to meet strict criteria which govern regular schools in terms of curriculum, organization and outcomes. In addition, they had to meet certain conditions laid down in order that integrated education has a chance of success.

The following criteria, likely to lead to successful integration, were studied by Dens *et al.* (1986):

1. The pupil's general intellectual ability should be at the same level as that of the average member of the group into which he or she is to be integrated.
2. The school attainment level should, at the very least, come up to the average level of the group.
3. The disabled child must have strong and sound motives for attending regular class.
4. He or she must show enough emotional stamina to cope in an ordinary school.
5. The home environment should provide sufficient and adequate support.
6. The ordinary school should have a positive general attitude towards the integration of the handicapped; the whole school team must be prepared to take special and appropriate measures.
7. The reception group should show sufficient openness; some appropriate preparation might be needed.

It appears from the analysis of survey results that 10 to 17 per cent of pupils had serious problems in meeting the general level of ability and school standards criteria required. This is particularly true of infant children, those with motor disabilities and pupils who enrol directly in integrated education.

The criteria regarding motivation, the ability to cope emotionally and family support were more readily met. Nevertheless, 16 to 22 per cent of them were still reported as being more or less problematic; we should perhaps conclude that real integration in these cases cannot be considered an undeniable success.

As far as positive attitude of the school and the openness of mind of the class group are concerned, 16 to 22 per cent of cases were reported to present problems. Considering the likely impact of these factors on the integration process, we believe that the recorded figures are distressingly high.

Progress achieved in school by integrated pupils

Retardation as compared to age On average, 20 per cent of pupils in integrated education presented a grade level retardation of two years or more; 52 per cent were one year behind in their schooling. In infant school, 31 per cent of pupils already presented one year's retardation. Pupils with motor disability were relatively slower in development. Moreover, the number of underachievers increased in the later years of primary schooling. At the secondary level, 85 per cent of pupils in integrated education were one year or more behind with their schooling. The question this poses is *when* exactly did these pupils slow down; in the special school or before they were admitted to special education.

The position of integrated pupils in their class group Integrated pupils are over-represented among the slowest 15 per cent of children within their respective class groups (see Table 1.5). In total, some 26 per cent of pupils in integrated education come under this 15 percentile level; 55 per cent of motor disabled pupils belong to this low-scoring group, and even pre-school children are greatly over-represented in this group.

Table 1.5 Integrated pupils within their class group

	Weaker 15%	Mean 70%	Strongest 15%
Total group	26		17
Motor handicap	55		6
Visual handicap	26		14
Auditory handicap	15		25
Origin regular education	30		13
Origin special education	18		26
Pre-school	38		7
Primary	22		16
Secondary (general)	21		31
Secondary (technical + vocational)	27		20

It is nevertheless interesting to note that, with the exception of the motor disabled and the pre-school children, pupils in integrated education are well represented among the successful pupils. Some 25 per cent of the hearing impaired score higher than the 85 percentile level. This is especially true for pupils who transferred from a special school. Does this indicate how carefully special education proceeds when returning its pupils to the mainstream? Of course, it could be that ex-special school pupils are under-rated, precisely on account of their past, and tend to be inserted at a lower level than their performance warrants.

Organizational aspects of support in integrated education

According to the relevant ministerial orders, integrated pupils should get at least weekly support from the special school which provides the support services. From the survey it appears that only a total of some 20 per cent received monthly (or even less frequent) support (see Table 1.6). The visually impaired and pupils in general secondary education rarely received their entitlement. This has to do with the notion that the support services provided within the framework of integrated education should come from a specialized establishment catering for the same type of disability as the pupil's own. What is more, support services for those with visual and hearing impairment are already scarce and the distance between the host school and the supporting school is often so great that the supportive visits take place at infrequent intervals (see Table 1.7). Because of this problem, much-needed coordination between all those involved is also eroded.

Only future experience will indicate the extent to which specialization will need to be maintained in order to organize integrated education in an educationally responsible and economically feasible way. The survey shows that, except for visual impairment, the other disability-related support services were only seen as such by no more than 50 per cent of members of

Table 1.6 Frequency of special interventions (in % of the number of pupils)

	Weekly	14 days	Monthly	Trimestrially/ occasionally
Total	59	17	8	12
Pre-school	59	29	6	6
Primary	57	18	10	9
Secondary	59	11	6	18
Motor handicap	67	10	3	3
Visual handicap	48	21	12	19
Auditory handicap	67	16	4	6

Table 1.7 Distances between regular school and special school (in % of the number of pupils)

	1–10 km	10–20 km	25–50 km	50 km
Total (%)	33	28	28	11
State schools	68.7	31.2	—	—
Municipal schools	65.9	14.9	19.2	—
Free schools	21.7	30	33.5	15

the guidance teams. In 22 per cent of cases, they believed that the support actually provided was also available in regular education.

Priorities of a future policy agenda

1. *Integrated education* will be extended to all types of special needs. As a result, different forms and levels of integration will come into existence. Along with *complete* and *permanent* integration, *partial* and/or *temporary* integration will also be made possible.
2. *Reintegration*, that is returning the special needs student to regular education, must be *further stimulated*. For some types of special needs it will be seen as the only option, namely for the mildly handicapped and the learning disabled.
3. *Consultation* and *coordination* remain central demands within the decision process. The *right of parents* to choose regular education for their disabled child will be respected, though the advantages made available by the law will be dependent upon the positive attitudes of the professionals concerned with assessment of special needs and programmes of implementation.
4. Special support should not only continue to be directed to individual pupils. Besides material or technical assistance to the regular school, the underlying *support of the teaching staff and the school* as a system is an important task for the specialist for integrated education.
5. *The setting of a time limit*, in accordance with the type and degree of the disability could possibly work as a stimulant, encouraging teachers within the mainstream to take on responsibility for planning and providing extra (special!) interventions for a full range of learners in the classroom.
6. *Training and continuing education for the teaching staff* of the regular schools and of specialized institutions, designed for particular tasks, remains the essential condition for the continuation of the integration 'movement'.

7. *Admission to integrated education must continue to be regulated.* Special provision must always be reserved for those who need it most. On the other hand, we must not limit the potential which every school has to search for special solutions which lie within its own realm of possibilities.

Conclusion

New approaches reinforce a concept of special education as an interim solution; indeed, a special school is seen as an early solution, but temporary and complementary to regular school education. The referral of pupils to this kind of special education is much less problematic than a 'street without end'. In this option, special education is seen as a necessity for many more children than there are now attending a special school. It is defined by a quality-based approach rather than by a territory-based label.

Another benefit is the integration of facilities, in order to make self-evident the integration of pupils. In such an integrated system, special education can be a real complement, an integral part of the whole system.

The role of the actual special school in the realization of this process is evident too. Special school staff members can make a positive contribution to the support of special needs pupils in the mainstream, and also to the development of the necessary school conditions to cope with their needs properly. In this way the basis of special education is not dominated by theories of disability, but on a respect for divergence between pupils. This is a more pupil-centred rather than school-oriented approach. It promotes a problem-solving attitude which is more directed towards negotiation and situation analysis than to the quick referral of the problem to someone else, perceived as a specialist in the matter (Diniz, 1989).

NOTE

1. PMS Centres: Psycho-Medical-Social Centres are regional guidance services, multidisciplinary teams, cooperating with, but independent from the school, responsible for the permanent guidance of the students. The activities are primarily intended to help pupils who are in a problem situation, but the centres also offer information about choice problems, and sustain the school team and the parents in their educational tasks.

CHAPTER 2

Denmark

Denmark is officially known as the Kingdom of Denmark and has a population of approximately 5 million. The official language is Danish. It is one of the smaller countries in the North of Europe which has taken a lead in its democratic response to the political wishes of parents and educationalists in the early 1960s with respect to integration.

One of the most fundamental principles of the educational policy in Denmark is that everyone, regardless of sex, social and geographical origins and regardless of physical or mental handicap, should have the same access to education and training. This goal has had a marked influence on Danish legislation on the educational front in recent years. In 1975, a new Education (Folkeskole) Act was passed which, in principle, established a comprehensive basic school from the 1st to the 10th forms.

In principle, all public education is free from the time a child is 5 or 6 years of age. This also includes teaching materials and equipment and the social and psychological help provided in the basic school, in the schools for the 16–19 year-olds and in some other institutions of education. Furthermore, in recent years, great importance has been attached to adult education, aimed at giving people who have been working since they were 14 or 16 an opportunity to supplement their skills.

Educational provision

The education system may be divided roughly into the main areas shown in Table 2.1

Today, everyone in Denmark has a basic education of nine years and about 85 per cent of the school-leavers enter some sort of continuing education.

Table 2.1 Educational provision in Denmark

Pre-school (age 0-6/7)	Day nurseries Kindergartens Pre-school classes Special pedagogical assistance to handicapped pre-school children		
Folkeskole (age 6/7–16/17)	1st–9th forms/ 10th forms		
	Vocationally-orientated education eg Apprenticeship training Basic vocational education courses (EFG) (8 vocational fields)	Academically orientated education, eg, Gymnasia, studenterkursus (2-year upper secondary level courses) and Higher Preparatory Examination (HF)	Youth and adult education, (age 14+) eg, labour market courses (retraining, continued and further education)
Youth education (age 16/17–19/20)	Basic examination courses at technical and commercial schools		Leisure-time education, Folk High Schools etc.
	Nautical training courses Government services training courses, e.g. within the Danish State Railways etc.		Single subject exam. courses for adults, (leaving exams of Folkeskole and HF, etc.)
Further education, age 19/20+	Further education courses		Municipal youth school

Primary and lower secondary education

The primary and lower secondary education provided by the Folkeskole is placed under the authority of the local governments and is free of charge. Since 1972, there have been nine years of compulsory basic education in Denmark, and most parents send their children to a Folkeskole (94 per cent of all children born in any one year attend this type of school). However, parents may, if they wish, have their children educated in other ways, ie, at private schools, which may receive up to 85 per cent of their running costs covered by the state. The Education (Folkeskole) Act of 1975, which came into operation in 1976, established a nine-year general basic education, covering the compulsory education age, with a supplementary optional tenth year and an optional pre-school class.

In principle the Folkeskole is comprehensive. However, in the 8 – 10th forms, pupils may, in certain subjects, choose between two courses of different content, namely a basic course and an advanced course. Pupils are also offered various optional subjects. For pupils in 8th and 9th forms, there are other ways in which they may complete compulsory education if they wish; ie, at a municipal youth school, a continuation school or, very frequently, and subject to permission from the School Board, by taking up employment.

The aim of the Folkeskole

First, the importance of cooperation with parents is stressed – something which has always been considered important in the Danish education system. For instance, all schools must appoint a School Board consisting of between five and seven parents. School Boards have various powers vested in them, regarding the teaching and administration of the school.

Second, it is emphasized that the aim of the Folkeskole is more than the mere conveyance of knowledge. It is recognized that the task of the Folkeskole is not solely to support and stimulate the intellectual development of the individual child, but also to take responsibility for the upbringing of the child. In this way the Folkeskole is also assigned a socio-educational role. Third, it is made clear that the pupils shall prepare themselves for life in a democratic society.

Special education and other special educational assistance in Denmark

Introduction

Until 1980 the responsibility for the education of the most severely handicapped children, youth and adults (approximately 1 per cent of the total number of students) was located within the Ministry of Social Affairs and regarded as solely a task of the State. But on January 1 1980 the principle of normalization of the conditions of the handicapped in the field of legislation was implemented in Denmark. This reform has been discussed and planned in a number of commissions and committees since 1964 and comprises a thorough revision of the overall social security system with substantial consequences in the social, health and educational sectors.

The basic incentive underlying this entire reform work lies in the finding that the previous social security system, based on legislation from 1933, did to a great extent ensure citizens in need of special support some qualified material assistance, but this was often done at an inappropriate, low level. In many cases society paid itself out of its responsibility towards weak citizens with cash or institutions on the implied condition that in return they were to keep to themselves with their equals. In Denmark in the 1960s with progress, optimism and prosperity, it was increasingly found in wider political circles that fellow human beings with social problems, more poorly endowed intellectually or with real handicap, might and should be included more in general human activity in education, work, leisure-time and housing.

The basic principles of special education

With the above mentioned fundamental intention as its basis, social reform was centred around three main principles: normalization, decentralization and integration.

Normalization is an expression common to all the efforts towards putting handicapped citizens on an equal footing with all other citizens in the society vis-à-vis legislation, administration and political authorities. Normalization is thus a challenge to society, *not* a wish or a demand for 'adapting' the individual to make him or her 'normal'.

Decentralization is a central part of the political/administrative development which took place during the 1970s in Denmark in all fields, and where the responsibility in as many fields as possible was transferred from the State to the 14 counties or as far down as to the 275 local authorities in the counties. It was attempted in the early 1970s to adapt the municipal structure to such a development, by joining small local districts to create political/administrative units sufficiently large to ensure the citizens a satisfactory level of service, but at the same time not so large as to make it impossible to establish a real grass-roots democracy.

Integration is a far more complicated and binding concept in relation to the prevailing administrative principles of normalization and decentralization, and can hardly be promoted *directly* through legislation; on the other hand, it may be impeded or prevented by the manner in which the legislation and the public administration of a nation are built up. Therefore, the three basic principles of social reform constitute a necessary whole, where the two first principles have been embodied in laws which in the long-run are to prepare the way for the last one.

The cancellation of all special laws (the mentally retarded, the deaf, the blind, etc.) is the expression of normalization, and now also the need for assistance and support of these handicapped groups, are satisfied under the provision of ordinary acts of parliament in the social, educational and health field. That is, all pre-school children are offered a place in kindergarten, all children's compulsory education is provided for under the Act of the Folkeskole or the Act on Private Schools, all sick people are treated on the basis of legislation relating to hospitals, etc. This legal normalization has entailed a number of administrations of the Danish handicap care service, previously under the Ministry of Social Affairs, being transferred to the ministries administrating the general legislation, now covering all fields. The previous responsibility of the Ministry of Social Affairs for the education of severely handicapped people has thus been transferred to the Ministry of Education. A great part of the administration of the previous special care has naturally remained within the sphere of the Ministry of Social Affairs.

The decentralization as from January 1 1980 has entailed almost all the previous state tasks, as far as the institutional assistance is concerned, being transferred to the counties, while individual (not given by institutions) assistance has been transferred to the local authorities.

In the field of education, the counties have taken over the previous obligation of the State to offer adults with physical or mental handicap remedial special education with the purpose of relieving or limiting the effects of the handicap, while in future the teaching of primary and lower secondary school pupils with severe handicap is to be provided for in financial, administrative and educational/psychological cooperation between county authorities and local authorities.

Integration has not been directly legislated for, and the only political decision on school integration is still a parliamentary resolution from 1969 to the effect: 'that the primary and lower secondary school should be expanded so as to provide for the teaching of handicapped pupils, to the greatest possible extent, in an ordinary school environment' (Hansen, 1989). However, legal normalization and administrative decentralization serve indirectly to promote integration, first because the abolition of the special acts of Parliament removed provisions which counteracted or even prevented integration (blind children, for instance were to be referred to a special boarding school run by the State), and second because decentralization meant that it was now the same authorities that were responsible for *all* pupils of primary or lower secondary school age, no matter whether they were mildly or severely handicapped, and consequently needed more or less extensive special support in education.

Consequences of reform in the educational sector

The transfer of the previous state teaching and educational obligations for handicapped people to the sphere of the Ministry of Education has resulted in an education system common to everyone, but with great possibilities for an efficient and individual programme.

Where the state special care service often called for grading, segregation and isolation on a group-diagnostic basis, the possibilities for organizing the required special support based on the handicapped individual's individual potential and need have now been considerably strengthened in a coherent, coordinated system.

The primary and lower secondary school

All children in Denmark of compulsory education age (7 to 16 years), from the ablest to the slowest learner, are now taught at primary and lower secondary schools (or at private schools which are run and financed differently, but provide instruction that in substance corresponds to that of primary and lower secondary school).

In addition to the nine years of compulsory education all children, if they (or their parents) so want, are entitled to one year in pre-school class and to continue in a tenth school year after compulsory education has ended. During this entire course from pre-school to the tenth form the school has to provide special instruction and other special educational assistance for pupils whose development requires special support.

In the Danish educational system the concept of special educational assistance includes the following four essential elements:

1. *Special instruction* – to ensure the handicapped student optimum qualifications from his or her schooling.
2. *Stimulation and training* – to develop reduced physical or mental functions as much as possible.
3. *Counselling/guidance* – to instruct the child's parents, teachers or other persons with whom the child is in daily contact, how to influence the child most effectively.
4. *Educational aids* – to reduce, technically, the adverse effect of the handicap on learning as much as possible.

The substance and organization of the special educational assistance are characterized by the following four aspects.

1. *Type of assistance*
   – concerning the educational programme called for by the handicap in question. In the Danish primary and lower secondary school special educational assistance is organized with a special view to the following disabilities which affect education:

> visual disabilities,
> hearing disabilities,
> motor disabilities,
> speech/language impairment,
> behaviour disorders,
> general learning disabilities and
> reading disorders.

2. *Form of assistance*
   – referring to the physical placing of the student in relation to the ordinary class (degree of integration). The primary and lower secondary school has at its disposal a very flexible and varied continuum of possibilities of how to place handicapped pupils, ranging from totally integrated special instruction in the class, to totally segregated special instruction at special boarding schools.
3. *Extent of assistance*
   – expressing the part of the weekly instruction which the student concerned receives as special instruction. The extent may vary from one, even a half lesson per week for a few weeks, to the entire instruction during the entire course of schooling.
4. *Nature of assistance*
   – indicating whether the local or the county authorities have the overall responsibility for the education of the student in question. Local authorities are to provide the *ordinary* special instruction, while county authorities are to provide the instruction if it is of an extensive nature, which presupposes:

> that the student is severely handicapped, or
> that the required special educational assistance cannot be given in the local district, or
> that expenses for the assistance considerably exceed the expenses for ordinary special instruction.

It should be noted, however, that the extensive special instruction under the auspices of county authorities are not free of charge for the local authorities; for each student referred, they have to pay an amount to the county authorities which on average corresponds to half the expenses for the extensive special instruction.

The implementation of the reform on January 1 1980 has meant that, in addition to providing special instruction, the primary and lower secondary school also offers children who have not yet started their schooling special educational assistance, if their development is considered to require this special support.

Previously, pre-school children – with or without handicap – solely represented a service responsibility for the social authorities (who of course still have such a responsibility), but in cases where it is a matter of an individual organized special educational effort with a view to relieving or limiting the difficulties for a pre-school child who is handicapped or whose development is at stake, the responsibility now rests with the school authorities.

Moreover, pupils with severe handicap have a special right to 11 years of schooling in the Danish primary and secondary school. The purpose of this provision is to give some of these students a greater chance of acquiring the qualifications necessary for passing the final examination in the lower secondary school, or, if this is not possible, to offer instruction which may strengthen these students as much as possible in their transition to adult life.

Perspectives of the reform

The Danish social reform has now been completed, and its consequences for the educational sector are visible in theory. Principles, intentions and statutory provisions are now to be realized in practice.

The will to fulfil a handicapped person's right to a permanent education in harmony with ordinary society is unmistakably present in the authorities, the politicians and the professionals concerned, but the economic situation does not favour these efforts. Whereas the social reform in Denmark was initiated and prepared in a period of prosperity and unlimited resources, it is now to be implemented in times of depression and economic decline.

The pedagogical-psychological assessment in relation to integration as far as the Folkeskole is concerned

Introduction

Realization of the fact that all children have a right to education is the first and most important element in the process known as 'pedagogical integration'. The question then arises: which place would be the best to teach children who have a handicap, that in one way or another, sets them apart from the average group of children constituting the school structure of any country?

Before trying to answer this question it is essential to keep some important points in mind:

- Children do not fall into one of two categories: 'handicapped' or 'non-handicapped'. In a group of children the ability to hear, see, think, move, etc. is present in varying degrees, ranging from the normal function, right down to total lack of function. Any distinction between 'handicapped' and 'non-handicapped' is therefore false!
- It would be untrue to say that the child's handicap in relation to the teaching situation consists of, and can be described as, simply a certain reduction of a certain physical or psychological function. A great deal of other and more important factors have to be taken into consideration when looking at the behaviour pattern which forms the basis of the child functioning at school. A person is more than a handicap!
- The difficulties a schoolchild may meet in the process of acquiring new information cannot exclusively be explained or understood by looking at the child's own functional inhibitions. The conditions and the teaching methods which the child is expected to respond to play a very large part and it is obvious that these factors vary a great deal from one age group to another, from school to school, from teacher to teacher, etc. A handicap is subject to change along with changing circumstances and demands made upon the child.

In the light of these various factors, it is considered impossible to integrate handicapped children on the grounds of group categorization, and absurd to talk about whether, for instance, mentally deficient children, deaf children or children with difficulty in learning to read should be integrated into a normal school class or not. It is essential to evaluate each single case. It becomes apparent that within the traditionally defined groups of handicap, there may be considerable differences in what would seem the most appropriate placing in the school for each individual child. Acknowledging this fact brings us close to saying, when it comes to an analysis of individual needs in the educational system, that the traditional division of handicap into groups is invalid and superfluous.

Placing handicapped children in school

In most countries which enjoy a well-organized school system, there are a number of children who do not derive maximum benefit from the standard education offered. These children are referred to different kinds of special support, known as 'special pedagogical assistance'. This assistance is first and foremost special education, but may involve the use of special pedagogical aids and assistance to parents, teachers or others outside the special pedagogical team who have a joint responsibility for the development of the child. It is quite common for 20 per cent of children attending school in the Western European countries to receive special pedagogical assistance during the entire, or part of the period they attend school. For some years the percentage has been increasing. This fact indicates that two closely related factors have made themselves felt at primary school level.

First of all, the demands in general for education at an ordinary level have been increasing, not only for the individual subjects taught, but also the range and variety of subjects covered. Next, the efforts to ensure that weaker children also derive reasonable benefit from their school years, for instance in the shape of special pedagogical assistance, has increased. However, all these children are, as already mentioned, handicapped to various degrees and in different ways. Therefore these children need special assistance of many different kinds.

The well-developed primary school system must therefore be extremely flexible and variable in its special pedagogical programme. It must be possible to offer special education (being more or less integrated or segregated depending on the child in question). The Danish special educational system may be used as an example to illustrate a system which is both flexible and varied. (See Table 2.2).

This continuum shows a series of various degrees of integration, ranging from total integration where the child attends a normal class, to total segregation, where the child is taught and lives at a residential institution. However, there are many alternatives between these two extremes, in this model of integration. The different possibilities indicate both a certain physical distance from a normal educational situation and a certain amount of the subjects given as special education. Groups made up of children who are in need of special education may, for instance, receive only *part* of their education in one or a few subjects, while in the Clinic of Education they receive *all* of their education in one or more subjects. In special classes established in connection with normal schools, there is a possibility of co-education with normal classes in certain subjects, while the special classes in special schools do not have this choice.

It is one of the most important tasks of the school to secure for each individual child in need of special education the type of support which caters precisely for the particular requirements of that very child.

Intake procedure of children to special education

When the special pedagogical support for a child is to be decided upon, prepared and specified, this normally happens in close collaboration with the teachers, the pedagogical psychologist and the parents. In many

Table 2.2 Various possibilities for giving handicapped children special education

Ordinary school with one extra teacher	One person in charge of the teaching	Special groups established in connection with a normal school	Clinic of special education at normal school	Special class established at the child's local school	Special class at a normal school outside the local school district	Special school department established in connection with a normal school (twin school)	Special school	Special boarding school or residential institution

increasing integration ← → increasing segregation

countries it is the pedagogical psychologist's responsibility to ensure that the necessary case investigation is carried out and the measures proposed are followed through. It must be stressed however, that at this stage collaboration with the teachers involved and the child's parents is of the utmost importance.

In countries where, for years, the principle of integration, in theory as well as in practice, has been a vital issue, a kind of programme of principles has been developed for the intake procedure of handicapped children to special education. In these manifestos it is largely agreed that the following five points must be kept particularly in mind:

1. *Proximity:* the child should attend school as close to home as possible.
2. *As little intervention as possible:* the child should not be offered more support or special education than absolutely necessary.
3. *Integration:* instruction of the handicapped child should take place in an ordinary and normal school environment if at all possible.
4. *Efficiency:* measures must be taken to ensure that the child derives maximum benefit from the subjects taught at school and thereby develops his or her own ability and talents to as large an extent as possible.
5. *Motivation:* it is essential that the special education established, and not least the degree of integration employed, is in accordance with what the teachers involved and the parents think is suitable for this particular child.

These principles do not constitute the key to a solution for the individual, concrete task of the intake procedure, but no procedure can take place without first considering these five points. It is obvious that the principles to a greater or lesser extent may clash with one another. Extensive integration for instance, is not always compatible with maximum efficiency in education, and the parents' wishes do not always accord with the school's idea of what is most beneficial for the child. The intake procedure is the process where a thorough evaluation takes into consideration the wishes of the teachers, the parents and the child.

The present situation in figures

In the Danish Folkeskole, special pedagogical support is offered to pre-school children, too. Figures show that during the years 1984/5 and 1985/6 between 3 and 4 per cent of all pre-school children received this kind of special support. In 1986/7 there was a marked increase with 4.25 per cent of pre-school children receiving special education (Ministry of Education, 1989). It would appear that most of the children, namely 77 per cent, were referred to special education owing to speech and language disabilities and

Table 2.3 Percentage of total primary school
pupils who are receiving special support

1981/2	12.92%*
1984/5	12.61%
1985/6	12.96%
1986/7	12.76%

*Including private schools

that about twice as many boys as girls are offered special teaching support. The percentage of the total number of pupils in primary schools who are receiving special support is shown in Table 2.3.

The absolute number of pupils receiving special education has been falling during the first half of the 1980s, but as the total number of pupils has been falling as well, the proportion of the two remained unchanged. It lies between 12 and 13 per cent.

Specific disabilities are the most essential reason why children get referred to special education. The education of most of the pupils takes place in normal classes, and often as clinic team-education. In Table 2.4 we can see the percentage of children who are considered to have special educational needs in each year of schooling. The smallest percentage of children is in kindergarten with almost 6 per cent of all pupils. This increases gradually up to almost 19 per cent in the 4th form, and starts a slow decline over the next six years to approximately 5 per cent in the 10th and 11th form. Pupils generally appear to be identified at 8–12 years of age as having more educational difficulties than their peers. As the numbers of pupils with special educational needs decline after that time, one can only conclude that educational intervention at the earlier stage leads to decreasing numbers of pupils experiencing difficulties in school.

Pupils with severe and multiple handicap

The majority of pupils are receiving special support in years 3–7 inclusive in schools, which is similar to other countries in Europe and can be linked to the forms of identification and means of resourcing used for pupils at different stages in their school career. Arguments have been presented both for integration and for segregation based on general philosophical considerations in Denmark. Extreme attitudes have periodically been widely fashionable and have given a certain exclusive character to the kind of special education a school could offer to those children in such need. For a period in the 1970s there was a widespread tendency for a change in views

Table 2.4 Percentage of pupils who received special education, recorded in 1st to 11th form.

	1981/2 % of pupils	1984/5 % of pupils	1985/6 % of pupils	1986/7 % of pupils
Kindergarten	7.1	5.87	6.02	5.97
1st Form	7.3	7.44	7.47	8.08
2nd Form	11.4	12.28	12.81	12.45
3rd Form	15.6	15.77	16.74	17.37
4th Form	17.5	17.47	17.81	18.65
5th Form	17.4	17.30	17.66	17.82
6th Form	17.5	16.69	17.31	17.19
7th Form	16.0	15.32	15.49	15.37
8th Form	12.0	10.47	11.24	10.63
9th Form	9.0	8.48	8.32	7.90
10th & 11th Form	10.4	6.72	6.70	4.94
In total	12.9	12.61	12.97	12.76

Source: Ministry of Education, 1989

in Denmark, but now it is apparent that a balance is establishing itself. It can be put like this: integration is a product of a serious and complex process which ought to ensure that *no child* is distanced further from a normal school environment than can be justified after careful consideration of the individual child's ability to derive benefit from education.

This viewpoint is offering a justification for separate schooling for pupils with severe and multiple handicaps in spite of the fact that Denmark is seen to lead the practice of integration in the EC. It is still considered difficult to integrate all pupils in ordinary schools. However, there are various practical ways that these pupils are integrated, socially and educationally, but as yet not fully integrated.

CHAPTER 3

France

France, officially known as the French Republic, is a country of approximately 55 million inhabitants. It is one of the largest countries in Europe and its official language is French. There are eleven years of compulsory schooling and in common with many other countries in Europe there are two parallel education systems, ordinary or mainstream education and special education.

The French school system is administered by the National Ministry of Education. There are eleven years of compulsory schooling from 6–16 years, although in recent years children have been provided with education from the age of 4 at nursery schools. Normally children begin school at 6 years old and complete two cycles of three years until transfer to secondary school at age 11 or 12. Secondary schooling is divided into college from 11–15 years and lycee from 15–18 years.

In secondary education students receive a general, technical and professional education and aim to take the Baccalaureat in one of these areas.

The education of pupils with special needs

The education of pupils with special needs is organized according to the principles of the Law of Orientation (1985). This law establishes a national obligation to educate 'handicapped' pupils as far as possible (de préférence) in ordinary schools; this applies to those who are able to be admitted in spite of their handicap. In this spirit, a political educational integration of young people with special needs has been progressing.

Another Orientation Law of Education in 1989 has reaffirmed the prime importance of educational integration in the professional and social integration of 'handicapped' children. In this spirit, local authorities have been encouraged by the Ministry of Education to develop whatever actions are necessary to allow the integration of 'handicapped' children and adolescents into ordinary schools in conditions which will be favourable to them. Different kinds of education are envisaged according to the nature and degree of the 'handicap':

a. *Individual integration*, full- or part-time in an ordinary class with psychological, pedagogic, medical or paramedical support.
b. *Education in special classes.*

Educational integration classes (formerly remedial and special classes) in different forms in certain primary schools or perhaps in nursery schools, welcome pupils with physical, sensory or mental handicaps who are able to benefit in an ordinary school, to an education adapted to their age and their capabilities and to the nature and the degree of their handicap. These classes operate according to the organizational advice given in 1991 to schools with pupils with special educational needs. Each class is limited to 12 pupils. The classes are taken by teachers who hold a special qualification entitled CAPSAIS (Certificate d'aptitude Aux Actions Pédagogiques Spécialisées d'adaptation et d'Integration Scolaires) which is a course for special teaching and educational adaptation in educational integration. There are also special personnel who take care of pupils and support them in ancillary school activities.

In secondary schooling ('colleges', in France), since 1965, there are the special needs sections (SES) and practical workshop classes which are integrated within the colleges and mainly cater for pupils who have attended special primary school classes, who are able to follow a general education, and to acquire a pre-vocational and vocational training.The SES are organized by and taught by specialized teachers and not by 'college' teachers.

c. *Full- or part-time admission into relevant special establishments.*

Special schooling takes place under the charge of 1) national education or 2) the Ministry of Social Affairs. 1) There are regional establishments for adaptive education (EREA) where pupils receive a parallel education similar to a school, a college, or a vocational school. 2) There are National institutes for deaf and blind pupils which give pupils and adolescents a general and vocational training provided by Ministry of Education staff. Institutes for sensory and motor re-education are managed by different associations, yet are also under the aegis of the Ministry of Social Affairs.

Medical education institutions are managed by the associations or by the local authority collectives in equal partnership with the Ministry of Social Affairs. They look after children and young people with learning difficulties (intellectual disability) who are often multi-handicapped and aged between 3 and 20 years and who need total care because of the seriousness of their handicap. The pupils who are not educated beyond the institution receive a general training according to the chosen focus of the establishment, either by teachers from ordinary and special schools or by private tuition approved and remunerated by the Ministry of Education. Pupils may also receive pre-vocational training from about 14 years of age.

National education inspectors who are responsible for educational adaptation and integration are also expected to evaluate the teaching on behalf of pupils with special needs, under the authority of the inspectorate and the directors of the departmental services of National Education.

Organization

Help for pupils

In the primary stage, special help is organized for pupils experiencing problems in basic education. The help needed for pupils is picked up initially by their teachers in different school settings. This help is augmented by the intervention of educational psychologists to assist, observe and understand the pupils' difficulties, to adjust the teaching and pedagogy and to evaluate the results. Special help is only provided when appropriate teaching is not carried out or when recourse to special help is obviously required right away. In this case, special help is put into place within the school. This help is organized by the special network for intervention under the responsibility of the national inspectorate: education psychologists, teachers from special schools and institutions (CAPSAIS) or option E (for pedagogic help), or option G (for re-education help).

Specialized help which is pedagogic must be organized:

- by restricting the numbers in classes for pupils with difficulties. These 'adaptation' classes must not contain more than 15 pupils, with the aim of reinstating pupils as quickly as possible into an ordinary class which can accommodate them.
- by regrouping temporarily, those pupils experiencing difficulties in classes where they are regularly enrolled. These groups are focused on pupils' specific pedagogic needs. Their manner of functioning is defined by the advice of teachers and written into the school plan which the head teacher guarantees. Numbers in such groups should not exceed 15 pupils.

Adaptation classes and groups are under the responsibility of the special full-time teachers of CAPSAIS (option E) who mainly operate in the same school. Special help which is re-educative is aimed at pupils with difficulties in nursery or primary schools.

Specialized intervention in every case is chosen in relation to the best methods and support available to professionals in the special network. Re-educative help is as far as possible put into place with the parents' support. With young children, intervention is made individually or in very small groups.

Numbers

In 1990/91, 16,130 handicapped children were integrated full-time in ordinary classes in public and private schools at primary level, and 65,916 children were included in 5,829 special classes in primary and nursery schools (public). There were 114,617 pupils included at secondary level into 1,621 special sections, and groups of practical workshop classes (public and private). Of the numbers of children in regional educational establishments (12,122 pupils in 1990/91),

- 7,733 or 63.8 per cent followed a vocational training programme,
- 3,855 or 31.8 per cent were in first-level classes in secondary schools,
- the remainder were either in the elementary level (3.6 per cent) or the second stage in general technology education (1.8 per cent).

Special education is the responsibility of the Ministry of Education which looks after pupils in special classes in ordinary schools or in special schools. The Ministry of Social Services and Solidarity is responsible for the establishments known as 'social education', 'medical educational' and 'medical' depending on the severity of the handicap, where in 1988/89 there were 139,649 pupils, of which 86,767 were at primary level.

The following relates to special education under the Ministry of Education. In primary schools, special pupils numbered 72,202 in 1988/89 which constituted 1.7 per cent of the total pupils in primary schools. There were 90 per cent of these pupils in special classes, mainly remedial classes, in ordinary schools. In 15 years the numbers of pupils in special schooling in primary schools has diminished by half, due to demographic reasons. In recent years, integration has increased in mainstream schools. Therefore, in 1988/89 there were 15,043 pupils, consisting of 9,517 with physical and sensory handicaps and 5,526 with learning difficulties who were integrated either individually or in groups into ordinary classes in primary schools.

In secondary schooling, there were 126,692 pupils in 1988/89 in special classes which represented 2.3 per cent of all pupils in early secondary education. Ninety per cent of these were mainly pupils with moderate learning difficulties who were relegated to special education sections (SES) and groups of practical/workshop classes (GCA) and were often integrated into ordinary secondary college classes. The remaining 10 per cent were pupils with profound or severe impairments like severe physical handicaps who attended special centres eg, the EREA (Regional Centres for Adaptive Training). In the same year, 8,274 pupils who had diverse handicaps were integrated into the ordinary secondary school.

The aims of the Ministry of Education and Social Affairs in the context of the educational integration of handicapped children and adolescents

Legislation (La Loi d'orientation) was passed in 1975 in favour of handicapped persons which instituted the educational obligation for handicapped children and adolescents to be integrated into ordinary schools as a priority. The integration circulars of 1982 and 1983 have developed various forms of action in schools to encourage further integration to take place.

The legislation on education in July 1989 takes into account the positive outcomes of these actions and makes a commitment to its development. The new plan for the primary school is the putting into place of cycles, differentiated forms of teaching, and the modification of teaching to fit the child's own rhythms which is seen to provide a more favourable context for active integration. The plan devised by the Minister of National Education is seen to translate these policies into effective measures for curriculum modification and educational integration.

The conditions will, in future, emphasize the policy of educational integration which assumes that the child and the adolescent have the right to be included and to be educated in the ordinary school. It is asserted by the Ministry of Education to bring to the school an enrichment of its aims in overcoming society's disadvantages. It encourages exchanges between pupils and students and the reciprocal recognition of differences. It creates favourable conditions for the amelioration of human and social relations and develops the notion of citizenship.

Integration into ordinary schools takes into account the school's aims and the pupil's capabilities. It is encouraged to take the form of a dynamic and positive process based on the real capabilities and potential of the young person, which supports the reasonable expectations of the families.

Forms of integration

The recognized right to education exerts itself either through education organized by the Ministry of Education, or in special establishments run by the Minister of Social Affairs and Integration.

In the absence of real difficulties, a refusal will not be made to the request for integration on behalf of a handicapped pupil, if the demand comes directly from the family or is made by an intermediary of a special establishment or service.

Two situations may arise. First, the teaching team, brought together by the head teacher or the director of the establishment, estimates the need for a pupil's educational integration. Immediate proposals are sent to the Special Education Commission, which is responsible for the notification of the integration proposed, and to ensure the putting in place of a pedagogic programme. The programme may be both educational and therapeutic, in liaison with the relevant services from national education eg, from a special educational establishment or service, from a paediatrician, psychiatrist, or from the voluntary sector.

Second, the teaching team, brought together by the head teacher or the director of the establishment, may estimate that the conditions for this integration are not effective. After having explained and justified this refusal to the initiator, the head teacher, or the director of the establishment, sends as soon as possible to the Commission of Special Education, a proposal for an 'adapted' response to the needs of the child or the adolescent:

- accommodation in a local school or establishment after which the conditions for a successful integration will be resourced and provided;
- accommodation in another educational school or establishment, with any special measures which are essential, eg, teaching, transport, etc.;
- accommodation in a special establishment with partial integration (part-time) in an ordinary school.

In each case, the responsibility for finding a solution to the teaching or the education of the child or the adolescent will not be left to the family alone.

The role of the special education commissions

These commissions guarantee the enactment of individual integration projects related to the 1983 circular. They advise and recommend to the administrative authorities, adaptations and developments for pupils which they view as useful in each individual case.

They also undertake the promotion of action for educational integration and ensure that the conventions put into place between the authorities, the local collectives and establishments, the special education services or the intervention from the voluntary sector, lead to many diversified actions in the establishment of integration practices.

Classes for educational integration

Classes for educational integration (les classes d'intégration scolaire [CLIS]) are a new concept in schools in France. The aim of the CLIS is to allow pupils to partly or totally follow the ordinary school curriculum. The CLIS now substitute for special classes, remedial classes, classes for sensory handicap, classes for motor handicap, etc. Many 'handicapped' pupils are directly enrolled in ordinary classes depending on whether the nature and degree of the handicap allows it, and if the conditions of their inclusion are fulfilled with reference to the integration circulars. These individual integrations will continue to be prioritized and are often supported by a peripatetic special teacher. The CLIS include children whose handicap has been recognized by a special education commission. The admission is dependent on the commission's decision. It is normal procedure for the consideration to be undertaken by the division of nursery and primary teaching (CCPE). In certain cases the decision of the departmental commission of special education (CDES) is required because the decision on admission is linked to the organization of specialized support with its particular financial implications. At the time of admission into a CLIS the special education commission requests the help of the teacher of the CLIS concerned, to seek advice about the composition of the class and of the teaching programme. The pupil admitted to the CLIS must be capable to some extent, of taking part in the life of the school, or alternatively, to acquire, or be in the process of acquiring, a capacity to communicate which is compatible with the teaching and the collective school life.

The pupil's situation is regularly revised in accordance with the 1976 circular related to the composition and function of special education commissions. Integration is followed up with a regular annual review of the situation. The CLIS counts as a class in the calculation of the number of classes in a school. Numbers in these classes are limited to 12 pupils.

Handicap

The analysis of the situation for 'handicapped' persons has been undertaken by the World Health Organisation (WHO) or in France the OMS which defines the theoretical and practical norms for deficiency, disability and handicap in the following manner:

- *an impairment* is a disruption of the anatomical, physiological or psychological structures or functions of the person;
- *a disability* affects the person by a limitation of the resulting functional possibilities, or the performance and restrictions in activities;

• *a handicap* is the disadvantage which results from the difference between what society expects of the individual, and what he or she is capable of doing considering his or her respective disability or impairment. For a given disability, the handicap is variable, partly related to social functions and partly to the help given to each person to lead a normal life. The norms defined by the OMS imply a positive approach to the situation for pupils admitted to the CLIS. This approach is particularly necessary in the work of educational training where it is seen as crucial to underline positive educational values.

The specific special teaching approaches used in the CLIS relate to the following objectives:

1) to use group dynamics with pupils;
2) to individualize the teaching objectives and procedures;
3) to limit the handicap and to increase autonomy;
4) to evaluate the results of the teaching.

1) Utilizing group resources is seen as fundamental, to allow the encouragement of expression and to set up and organize good communication and collective means to work in school.

2) Adaptation of the teaching procedures for each pupil is important to allow each pupil to have an individual programme, which defines aids and technological equipment, special techniques and an evaluation of the results obtained. It takes the form of a written document, in liaison with the family, which can be readjusted, if necessary, and records progress and procedures applicable to each pupil.

3) Utilizing technological aids is increasing being encouraged to reduce or limit the handicap, especially in the field of sensory and motor handicap, to prepare for the control of communication and information techniques, eg, calculators, magnetoscopes, minitel, etc. Personal expression in the creative development of pupils related to music, video, etc., is also encouraged.

4) A practical form of evaluation is seen as essential to analyse the results obtained by pupils. This is predominantly the responsibility of the teacher, to build in some form of evaluation into the teaching procedures. It is the role of the inspectorate (l'inspecteur de l'éducation nationale [IEN]) to undertake institutional evaluation and critical examination of the function of the CLIS and the results obtained, as well as the inspection of teachers of the CLIS.

In reviewing the present situation with respect to pupils with special needs in France, it is interesting to note some further facts. In 1990 there were 273,392 pupils taught in remedial or specialized classes and establishments in metropolitan France, and 10,500 pupils in overseas establishments (Ministere de l'Education Nationale et de la culture, 1991). The profile of pupils in special education shows that:

- the number of boys outnumbers that of girls;
- half of the 'taught' pupils are 12–15 years of age;
- the numbers of pupils leaving school at 16 years of age have decreased since 1987/8.

In relation to pupils educated through the different government ministries, 190,870 pupils receive help in educational establishments run by the Ministry of Education, and 86,827 are in special schools run by the Ministry of Social Affairs (1990/91).

We see in 1989/90 a drop in the strength of pupils in all establishments under the responsibility of the Ministry of Education. There are 5,042 pupils in Metropolitan France and 5,135 pupils for France (without overseas territories). In secondary schooling in specialized public and private education and in workshop classes there has been a drop of approximately 3,000 pupils. In regional educational establishments with special support, numbers remain stable.

The special education sections (SES) and the practical workshop classes (CGA) are organized to:

- receive, after ordinary primary schooling or remedial teaching, those pupils with learning difficulties. There are equal numbers of pupils who have failed academically and pupils with behaviour problems.
- give adolescents a general education and a professional training. The objective is to allow pupils access to further education.

The remedial classes are not taken into account with remedial teaching and the network of support helpers play a role in the maintenance of ordinary teaching for students who are failing in elementary schooling. In 1989/1990 there were 2,645 specialized support workers in metropolitan France and 63 overseas (as against 2,605 and 55 in 1988/89).

Boys always outnumber girls

Of those taught in special education, 166,057 were boys and 107,335 were girls; boys were, therefore, 60.7 per cent of the total and are in the majority at all ages (see Table 3.1).

The proportion of pupils 'taught' in special education varies according to age, from 0.3 per cent at 5 years to 4.0 per cent at 13 and 14 years of age. The distribution by age of the numbers of pupils in special education

Table 3.1 The distribution of pupils taught in special education by age and gender 1990/91

Age	Boys Numbers	%	Girls Numbers	%	Boys and Girls Numbers	%
5	1,232	60.1	819	39.9	2,051	100
6	1,717	61.4	1,079	38.6	2,796	100
7	3,824	61.6	2,388	38.4	6,212	100
8	8,234	61.2	5,211	38.8	13,445	100
9	11,800	61.1	7,212	37.9	19,012	100
10	13,723	61.3	8,655	38.9	22,378	100
11	13,831	61.4	8,678	38.6	22,509	100
12	17,770	61.3	11,221	38.7	28,991	100
13	21,314	60.9	13,675	39.1	34,989	100
14	21,245	60.9	13,626	39.1	34,871	100
15	21,120	60.4	13,863	39.6	34,983	100
16	13,583	58.6	9,580	41.4	23,163	100
17	8,258	59.7	5,578	40.3	13,836	100
18+	8,406	59.4	5,750	40.6	14,156	100
Total	166,057	60.7	107,335	39.3	273,392	100

consistently presents the same characteristics, particularly in the age group 12–15 years which represents 50 per cent of the total number of pupils in special education in contrast to the 5–6 year olds who only represent 1.7 per cent of the total. As is generally the trend in other European countries, the numbers of pupils identified with special learning needs increase in the secondary school phase, between the ages of 11–15 years. This is largely related to the means of identifying special needs in children at different ages, and recording the data.

For integrated pupils, direct admissions are predominant

Primary level

If we look at Table 3.2 we see that in metropolitan France there are 16,385 pupils who are taught in ordinary schools full-time; 86.2 per cent are educated in public establishments and 13.8 per cent are in private establishments of different kinds.

Of these pupils, 43.2 per cent are admitted into the ordinary school after having a departmental special education commission (CDES) and 56.8 per cent are admitted directly. Pupils admitted by the commission are pupils who are designated as having:

Intellectual impairment 48.4%
Motor impairment 19.4%

50

Table 3.2 Primary school pupils with special needs in the ordinary school according to the type of handicap

	Pupils admitted after a departmental special education commission			Pupils directly admitted			Part-time pupils in primary school	
	Public No.	Private No.	%	Public No.	Private No.	%	Public No.	Private No
Blind	64	6	1.0	61	10	0.8	41	2
Visually impaired	533	12	7.7	520	135	7.0	112	4
Deaf	681	78	10.7	776	194	10.4	455	9
Hearing impaired	222	27	3.5	439	168	6.5	67	9
Motor impairment	1,243	133	19.4	2,379	508	31.0	438	52
Emotional problems	568	89	9.3	1,270	282	16.7	467	30
Intellectual impairment	3,148	275	48.4	2,222	342	27.6	1,011	82
Total	6,459	620	100	7,667	1,639	100	2,591	188
	7,079			9,306			2,779	
Grand total							16,385	

Emotional problems	9.3%
Deafness	10.7%

Pupils who are admitted directly present similar problems, viz:

Motor difficulties	31.0%
Intellectual difficulties	27.6%
Emotional difficulties	16.7%
Deafness	10.4%

Again we observe a similar pattern of pupils' difficulties in referrals. There is a majority of pupils with learning difficulties in need of special educational help, yet there are also high numbers of pupils with physical and sensory difficulties integrated together in the ordinary school.

In France it is still the tradition to employ different Ministries to educate or care for pupils and children with special educational needs. However, it is clear that the policy of encouraging integration is followed by both Ministries separately and together in the furtherance of this ideal. The Ministry of Social Affairs and Integration is responsible for the medical, medical/educational and social educational centres, where children and young people with severe disabilities or learning difficulties are 'accommodated'. Not all of these pupils are offered educational schooling. The majority of pupils in these centres are accepted or welcomed; in 1989/90 these totalled 138,084, whereas just over half of this number – 86,626 – are educated or taught by qualified teachers.

Table 3.3 Teaching structures for remedial and special education

	SECONDARY			
Ordinary classes in colleges and schools	←	Remedial classes in colleges (SES and GCA)	←	Remedial classes in local schools EREA
	PRIMARY			
Ordinary classes in colleges and schools	←	Remedial classes in ordinary schools	←	Remedial classes in special schools
	PRE-PRIMARY SCHOOLING Individual school integration			

Source: Ministere de l'Education Nationale, 1991

Finally, we can see from the overview of the French teaching structures for remedial and special education in Table 3.3, how the teaching for pupils in the centres is split between the ordinary school, the special school, the centre or the hospital, depending upon the placement of the pupil and the severity of the disability. We can also see the clear distinction between establishments run by both ministries and the progression and possible interchange of pupils from school to school and from class to class within the education system.

France is making clear efforts to bring as many pupils as possible into the mainstream by passing enabling legislation, providing new support structures for special provision in ordinary schools, and in publishing documentation for all professionals in education in an attempt to change the views and attitudes of the existing educational establishment. A rigourous review and research of the practice will establish whether or not the new directives and processes of inter-school exchange and the inclusion of pupils in the mainstream is working. The future of schooling in the country is in the hands of the professionals with the goodwill to see it through, and the resourcing of educational managers to provide the financial re-organization necessary for its success.

CHAPTER 4

Germany

Today the Federal Republic of Germany is a federation of 16 länder or states. Before October 1990, the FRG consisted of 11 states; since that date five new ones, from the former East Germany have been added. The total population of the FRG is 79 million people including foreign workers (Federal Ministry of Education and Science, 1992). The responsibility for education policy and planning is governed by the Federal State structure. Whereas the Bundesländer have been given 'general competence' for education, the Federal Government has only limited legislative and financial powers, and may participate in educational planning. There are ten years of compulsory schooling in Germany and German is the official language. The Government allows freedom of movement and free choice of teaching career anywhere in the FRG provided that the implementation and realization of cooperation is supported by the Federal State legislation.

General education in Germany is developed within five phases: pre-school education, primary education, secondary education at stage 1 and stage 2, and higher and continuing education. All children in the FRG who have reached their sixth birthday are obliged by law to attend school. As a general rule, compulsory school attendance lasts nine or ten years, depending on the Federal State concerned. The first four (or in some cases, six) years of schooling take place at a primary school (Grundschule) and the remainder in a secondary school (Weiterführende Schule). On completion of class 4 (or 6) pupils move onto main school (Hauptschule) for five years or to intermediate school (Realschule) for six years or to grammar schools (Gymnasium) for nine years. The compulsory attendance at school on a daily basis for nine years is followed by three years' compulsory attendance at a vocational school (Berufsschule) on a part-time basis, usually once a week. The rest of the week is given to practical training in a business or firm.

Special schools

Special schools are called 'Sonderschulen' in German. Developments with regard to special schools have been largely synchronized over the last two decades as a result of an agreement reached by the Education Ministers Conference (the Standing Conferences of the Education Ministers of the Federal States [KMK]) in 1960. The agreement contained a report on policy for special schools, and recommendations on the 'Pattern of the Special School System' was further agreed in 1972. The legal basis for special education is similar in all the Federal States. The right to suitable education and training is laid down in the individual constitutions of the Federal States and set out in the various educational laws. Compulsory school attendance extends to handicapped children and adolescents. The policy in all federal states is, wherever possible, for handicapped children to be in the ordinary school. Special schools, however, are provided when considered to be necessary.

In the FRG generally, great effort is put into the prevention of early disability by the provision of early intervention programmes. Every child is entitled to 13 medical and psychological developmental check-ups by a paediatrician, beginning at birth up to the age of 9 years. If therapy or special help is needed for the child it will be given by local medical, psychological or educational institutions, eg, University clinics, child guidance centres or private therapy. This therapy is paid for by the State or by Social Services. In the past ten years, many kindergartens with an 'integration' focus have been established which offer special educational programmes and therapy for children with special needs. At present the situation in relation to 'integration' in the FRG is difficult to assess, because there is no general framework for its development and no coordinated programme for the development of mainstreaming (or inclusion in ordinary schools). The special school system has a long tradition in the FRG and its effectiveness is highly valued within the educational system (Randoll, 1991).

Special schools are designed to provide education and training for children and young people who are capable of attending school, but because of a particular physical, mental or psychological difficulty are not able to take advantage of ordinary school facilities. Special schools are divided into categories relating to the particular requirements of the pupils concerned and operate on special educational principles. Special schools exist for those pupils:

- who are blind;
- who are deaf;
- who are mentally handicapped;

Table 4.1 Pupils in special schools in Germany

	1980	1985	1986	1987	1988	1989	1990
Pupils	353,867	270,999	261,062	253,978	248,011	246,080	251,705
Classes for learning disabilities	243,931	163,580	152,740	143,280	136,422	131,589	133,102
Other disabilities	109,936	107,419	108,322	110,698	111,491	114,491	118,603
Blind	1,327	1,165	1,066	983	1,277	1,137	1,118
Visual impairment	2,654	2,341	2,226	2,129	2,016	2,001	2,048
Deaf	4,039	3,238	3,053	2,907	2,734	2,622	2,370
Partial hearing	6,575	5,757	5,412	5,049	4,834	4,819	4,950
Speech impairment	14,316	17,841	18,726	19,461	19,879	20,946	22,168
Physical handicap	13,702	13,738	13,244	13,526	13,613	13,873	13,116
Mental handicap	46,339	41,504	40,436	38,869	37,970	37,013	33,394
Emotional problems	9,755	8,533	8,571	8,720	8,788	8,993	9,330
Ill or delicate	4,797	5,372	6,153	7,512	7,453	7,438	6,861
Multiple handicap/ and home education	6,432	7,930	9,435	11,542	13,025	15,649	23,248

Schule Statistik, 1991

- who are physically handicapped;
- with learning difficulties;
- with impaired hearing;
- with impaired vision;
- with impaired speech;
- with behaviour problems;
- with health problems.

The number of special schools in Germany was approximately 3,070 in 1991 and the majority of these schools (1,500) were for pupils with 'learning disabilities'. Table 4.1 shows the categories of pupils in the special schools.

We find that there are 251,705 pupils presently (1990) in attendance at special schools; 166,496 pupils or 66 per cent of these pupils are categorized as learning disabled and mentally handicapped, which is a very high percentage. However, we can also see from the figures that the pupil numbers in special schools have decreased in the last ten years by approximately 100,000 pupils or 28 per cent of the total in 1980. The main decrease has been in the area of 'learning difficulty'. Other categories of handicapped pupils have also decreased slightly in the same period with the exception of pupils with speech impairment and who are chronically ill – these categories have increased slightly.

Table 4.2 illustrates the way that classes are organized in special schools. The table shows that there are 39,709 teachers available for 25,637 classes. The average class size in special schools is 9.8 pupils, although the average for pupils with learning difficulties is slightly higher at 11.6 and classes for pupils with other disabilities is 8.4. The

Table 4.2 Classes in special schools

	1980	1985	1986	1987	1988	1989	1990
Total classes	29,911	26,791	26,302	26,002	25,436	25,606	25,637
For pupils with learning disabilities	17,095	13,543	12,874	12,346	11,797	11,484	11,497
Other disabilities	12,816	13,248	13,428	13,656	13,639	14,122	14,140
Teachers for learning disabilities	21,720	18,588	18,032	17,330	16,906	16,343	16,505
Other disabilities	19,259	21,212	21,779	21,635	21,942	22,578	23,204
Pupils in class	11.8	10.1	9.9	9.8	9.8	9.6	9.8
For learning disabilities	14.3	12.1	11.9	11.6	11.6	11.5	11.6
Other disabilities	8.6	8.1	8.1	8.1	8.2	8.1	8.4
Teacher/pupil ratio	8.6	6.8	6.6	6.5	6.4	6.3	6.3
For learning disabilities	11.2	8.8	8.5	8.3	8.1	8.1	8.1
Other disabilities	5.7	5.1	5.0	5.1	5.1	5.1	5.1

teacher:pupil ratio in special schools generally is 6.3 on average, which is again unevenly distributed between schools for learning disabled pupils at 8.1, as compared to 5.1 in schools for pupils with 'other disabilities'. The table also illustrates that in the last ten years the number of pupils per class has decreased overall in all special schools from 11.8 to 9.8, and that the teacher:pupil ratio also shows a favourable decrease from 8.6 to 6.3 generally in all special schools.

There is a high percentage of pupils categorized as having 'learning difficulties'. This group comprises 53 per cent of the total group in special education generally. If this group is combined with pupils with 'mental handicap', the combined total for the two groups is 66 per cent of all pupils in special schools. This illustrates two important factors: a) that special school pupils comprise 4 per cent of all pupils in schools in the FRG; b) that there has been an overall decrease in the numbers of pupils in special education in the FRG.

Other conclusions from the previous tables are that: c) pupil numbers have decreased in the last decade, partly due to demographic reasons; d) there has been a gradual transferral of many pupils with learning difficulties into ordinary schools as part of a process of integration; and e) pupil:teacher ratios in special schools are very favourable and have decreased in the last decade to the present 1:6.3 pupils.

In the last decade the question of the integration of pupils with special needs in the FRG has become more important. In eight federal states, first steps have been taken to educate handicapped children in ordinary schools. In four of these federal states, integration projects have developed to such an extent that parents of handicapped children have the right to decide whether their child should be educated in a special or an ordinary school.

There have been different concepts of integration adopted in the different states. There is the concept of:

- integration as 'differentiating the instructional objectives' in the ordinary classroom. Pupils are given differentiated teaching in the ordinary school;
- individual integration of pupils with the support of peripatetic teachers and an individual educational programme, to reach the achievements of the ordinary school curriculum;
- integration through the cooperation of schools, usually between a primary and a special school, with the intention of preventing pupils who are beginning school from developing difficulties in learning and social behaviour. The cooperation may involve special teachers advising the teachers in the ordinary school about problems they are experiencing with pupils;
- integration as a school project. Each class with special needs pupils has two teachers, one ordinary class teacher and a special teacher. Each class has a maximum of 20 pupils, five of whom are pupils with special needs. This could be named 'parallel integration' ie, integration in parallel classes in certain chosen primary schools.

In furthering integration in the FRG, parents, teachers and academics are making efforts to include handicapped children wherever possible into ordinary schools in all the Bundesländer (states). The state of Hesse has introduced new legislation which basically allows the integration of handicapped pupils into ordinary schools, provided there are no objections on serious medical or organizational grounds. The Landesregierung (State Government) in Weisbaden, the state capital, was so surprised at the response from parents of handicapped children that it was obliged, initially, to impose restrictions on enrolment in ordinary schools at the beginning of the new school year. The parents of over 1,000 handicapped children had opted for the integration of their children into the ordinary school system. The Education Minister in Weisbaden had to restrict the numbers of pupils because of lack of staff, experience, qualifications and finance for the project. Children were considered who had previously been in their first or second school year, or those who had attended pre-school. However, the integration of handicapped children is to be considerably expanded next year (BW, 1991b).

There are also 1,510 handicapped children who are being taught in 248 ordinary schools in the state of Northrhine–Westphalia. Similar to the practice in other länder, a specially trained remedial school teacher assists during lessons. All school pilot projects have met with a surprisingly marked positive response. The front-runners in integration appear to be the primary schools (Grundschulen) and the comprehensive schools (Gesamtschulen).

Pilot schemes with integrated classes were also approved in lower Saxony at the beginning of the school year. In all, in this state, 84 children now share the same lessons in 29 integrated classes in ordinary schools (Grundschulen and Hauptschulen) and in a few diagnostic classes (Orientierungsstufen) (BW, 1991b).

Agreements between the Federal States on standardization in the educational field, particularly those concluded in 1954 and 1964, have provided the basic structures of the education system in the States, with a large measure of uniformity, particularly in such things as the length of compulsory schooling, the beginning and end of the school year, the length of school holidays, the designation of the different types of educational facilities, their organizational form, the sequence in which languages are taught and the evaluation of scholastic achievements. With further supplementary agreements by the KMK, the mutual recognition of examinations and certificates, as well as a number of other harmonizing elements within the educational system were achieved, while simultaneously setting out the required standards. These agreements play an important part in the amalgamation of different state systems in the reunification of the FRG (BW, 1991a).

There is a well-established and resourced special school system in Germany, designated according to the child's major 'handicap'.

Schools for the blind

Schools for the blind are attended by children and adolescents who have no sight or have major sight loss, ie, pupils whose acuity of vision does not exceed 1/50 of the norm, or where other sight defects of the same degree exist. Learning processes, in which visual perception plays an important part, take place with the assistance of special aids and methods eg, Braille.

Children and young people with severely impaired vision are also accepted, with an acuity of vision between 1/20 and 1/50 of the norm, or when their eyesight has other defects to the same degree of severity. As a general rule, pupils are dependent on blind instruction media and methods in educational and training situations, and aids for the blind in daily life.

Schools for children with impaired vision

Schools for pupils with impaired vision admit pupils who cannot be satisfactorily educated in ordinary schools. Pupils in this category are often those

58

who, despite corrective glasses, have a central acuity of vision of 1/3 or less in the better or both eyes, or whose eyesight is impaired to a serious degree.

This calls for special forms of teaching and learning, using special technical and learning aids. The choice of the most suitable type of school for pupils who have other handicaps in addition to impaired eyesight, is made on an individual basis.

Schools for deaf children

Schools for the deaf admit pupils who have been deaf from birth, or pupils who became deaf before learning to speak. Children are also accepted who become deaf at a later date, but who do not possess the same faculty of speech as their peers. These schools also accept pupils with remnants of hearing whose speech development, despite the use of aural aids from an early age, clearly indicates that they are not equal to the speech requirements of schools for children with hearing impairment. Children who are mentally handicapped and who are categorized as having learning difficulties are taught in special classes or departments in schools for the deaf.

Schools for children with hearing impairment

Children and young people are admitted to schools for hearing impairment if their hearing is affected in such a way that, even with hearing aids, they cannot be educated at an ordinary school in accordance with their abilities, and who need special teaching processes and educative measures to overcome or reduce their disability. The procedure which allows children admittance to a school for hearing impairment, or transfer from such a school to another school is laid down in regulations issued by the respective Federal State.

Schools for children with mental handicap

All mentally handicapped children, regardless of the manner and severity of their disability, must be included in promotional educational programmes. Schools for the mentally handicapped are designed for pupils whose learning behaviour and stage of development are considerably below what may be expected as far as age is concerned. They are pupils who will not receive sufficient help at school for pupils with learning difficulties.

Different degrees of learning ability and different types of learning behaviour can be established according to the extent of the disability. By applying suitable measures designed to stimulate and improve learning behaviour, great progress is possible during the course of a promotional educational programme. In certain cases there may be pupils with outstanding ability in some areas, and marked deficits in others.

Schools for children with learning difficulties

Children and adolescents are regarded as having learning difficulties if they have a prolonged learning difficulty which deviates quite markedly from their peers in standard achievement and behaviour. These pupils are unable to receive educational promotional measures to meet their requirements from the special learning assistance provided in primary and other ordinary mainstream schools. There is also the broad area of 'generalized learning disturbances' which may turn into learning handicap through unfavourable interaction. Extensive and lengthy learning failure may emerge with different behaviour and achievement structures. Generalized learning disturbances can only be assumed if there is evidence of extensive and prolonged learning failure.

Problematic circumstances in the family, school or environment may activate emotional disturbances, learning handicaps and unacceptable behaviour which may lead to general or lasting failure in school. This may result in many pupils failing in ordinary school requirements, although their intellectual level is not always appreciably impaired in any way.

Schools for children with physical handicap

Schools for pupils with physical handicap admit pupils who experience restricted movement and specific organic damage. If these disorders interfere with dealing with school practical materials or the completion of school work in an ordinary or other special school, then pupils will be individually assessed for admittance. Schools for the physically handicapped provide special programmes for pupils:

- who require help and nursing care to a considerable extent, eg, pupils with acute cerebral motoric disturbances who are dependent on others for basic daily necessities;
- whose emotional and social development has not reached the stage where they can be taught in a group over long periods. This may occur as a result of severe general development disorders or multiple disablement, or as the result of serious social disturbances in the case of minor motoric restriction, eg, restless, disturbed physically handicapped children;
- whose maximum stress level has been reduced as a result of a serious handicap or a severe organic disorder which only allows them to take part in instruction for short periods.

Schools for children with speech impairment

Children with impaired speech are considered eligible for special school education when their handicap is so serious that they cannot be adequately assisted by help in an ordinary school or by a course of treatment for a limited period.

Generally, handicaps of this nature represent marked underdevelopment of speech with symptoms of multiple or universal stammering or other speech impediments. The numbers of children attending these schools can be considerably reduced by intensive pre-school and speech therapy.

Pupils with impaired hearing or vision, with physical, learning or mental handicaps who have speech defects usually attend the respective schools. Speech therapy measures are also provided at these other special schools. Pupils with only a slight speech impairment are expected to remain in ordinary schools where they receive the necessary therapeutic treatment. Pupils are transferred from schools for children with speech impairment to other special schools if it is thought that the school will provide better educational measures to help the child.

Schools for children with behaviour problems

Those schools providing corrective education. Special educational assistance is necessary in schools for children with behavioural disturbance if the symptoms of the disorder cannot be overcome by general educational and institutional means or by peripatetic help because of their variety, duration, incidence or intensity.

Physically, mentally or sensorially handicapped pupils who also show maladjusted behaviour are not normally admitted to these schools; relative measures are adapted for them at the special school concerned. The combination of disturbed emotions and social conspicuousness occurs frequently. Even in the case of average or above-average intelligence, the scholastic achievement level of behaviourally disturbed pupils is frequently poor because they can only be occasionally motivated to learn in school, if at all.

Schools for ill and delicate children

Children and adolescents of school age who are hospitalized because of an illness of some duration, can receive school instruction within the limits of what doctors consider is acceptable for the patient. The structure of a hospital school and the teaching undertaken depends largely on the type of hospital. Three kinds of hospital can be identified: general hospitals, recuperation and rehabilitation hospitals, and psychiatric and psychosomatic clinics. If the pupils cannot come to the hospital school-room, the teacher goes to his or her bedside.

The number of lessons received by pupils in these schools amounts to 12 per week. When deciding the extent of such instruction, medical and educational requirements must be weighed up and taken into consideration. To ensure that sick pupils can be systematically helped as much as possible, hospitals contact the school previously attended and maintain contact during the pupils' hospitalization. The schools are also consulted on the issuing of reports and promotion to the next class. The help offered by hospital schools is not of a purely scholastic nature; responsibilities often go beyond those of teachers in normal schools. Seriously ill children derive great hope from the attention of the hospital teacher. The teaching can positively affect the success of the treatment.

Early intervention measures

Children in their infancy or early childhood who, following a medical diagnosis, have a possible handicap, can receive special pedagogical care at this early age at the wish of the parents via advice centres which are, in some cases, located in special schools. The purpose of these advice centres is to diagnose handicaps at as early an age as possible and to overcome or prevent them. In addition, the parents concerned receive advice and are given guidance on how they should deal with their handicapped child.

These special pedagogical advice centres are part of the overall special system. Experts who have undergone special pedagogical training (particularly special school teachers) work in close cooperation with educators, physical therapists and medical services at these advice centres. The assistance and special programme provided by the advice centres is free of charge for the parents. Special help for the child and advice for the parents can also be given at home within the programme of house visits.

Children who, because of their particular ability, seem to be in need of special care before they commence school, can, with the agreement of the parents, attend special kindergartens on completion of their third birthday (after the second birthday in the case of physically handicapped children). These institutions are specialized in the various types of handicap.

The groups are looked after by a female educator (Erzieherin). Special school staff also assist. On reaching the age of compulsory school attendance, each child is examined to establish whether he or she is in need of the educational programme provided by a special school or whether the child can attend a normal school.

62

Educational intervention measures

All educational courses which the school system offers non-handicapped pupils are available at the above-mentioned special schools, provided this is appropriate for the child's disability. Schools for children with impaired hearing, for instance, offer main school (Hauptschule), intermediate school (Realschule) and grammar school (Gymnasium) educational courses. This means that pupils attending special schools can (depending on ability) acquire a main, intermediate or higher school certificate, ie, Abitur. To quote a second example, schools for the physically handicapped also offer curricula culminating in all the final certificates which can be acquired at normal schools in the FRG. These schools provide classes suitable for both the physically and mentally handicapped. There is also a special department for physically disabled and educationally subnormal pupils. All other children and young persons attending schools for the physically handicapped have the opportunity of educational programmes leading to main and intermediate final certificates, as well as Abitur.

In other words, attendance at a special school does not mean that handicapped children and young persons are deprived of the opportunity of final secondary school certificates. On the contrary, the educational programmes at special schools are designed for the pupils so that they can obtain these secondary school qualifications. In this way they are enabled to avail themselves of the opportunity of qualifying for vocational training or higher educational study courses.

Special schools also have the responsibility of promoting those pupils in question to a point where they can go to a normal school. A relatively large number of pupils at schools for impaired speech and those providing corrective education are transferred to normal schools – eventually. This also applies to schools for children with learning problems where many children return to normal schools.

Numerous pilot schemes are attempting cooperation between primary, main and special schools; the framework and conditions for joint instruction of handicapped and non-handicapped children are also being examined. All these pilot schemes are aimed at improved integration of handicapped young persons in school and society.

Federal Government report

In its 1984 report on 'The State of the Handicapped', the Federal Government states that the promotion of handicapped children and juveniles of pre-school and school age must be viewed in a markedly differentiated manner. The report states:

Education has a special significance for handicapped persons. On the one hand it gives them the opportunity to develop their personality on their own responsibility, and on the other, the vocational and other opportunities of handicapped children and young persons depend to a much greater measure on the quality of training and final certificates than they do for the non-handicapped. All handicapped persons must be enabled to develop their own individual ability and inclinations.

Sustained efforts by the Federal States and the Federal Government have, since the late 1960s, resulted in an improvement in the educational opportunities of handicapped children and young persons.

The Federal Government of Germany now has a well-developed and efficient special school system. Over 600 special kindergartens providing a total of 17,000 places cover different individual needs; some 2,800 schools for the handicapped are educating approximately 320,000 pupils. In almost 500 special school kindergartens, just under 9,000 disabled children are being prepared for subsequent school attendance.

However, the pattern of education in special institutions at the present time has become the subject of ever-increasing criticism. Special schools are often regarded as 'schools for the leftovers' with reduced opportunities and, as a consequence, they are being rejected; the isolation of special school pupils is criticized on the grounds that it results in a hardening of prejudices towards the handicapped. In order to counter the danger of unnecessary 'protected areas' and isolating special conditions, and to put into practice the principle of 'As much assistance as necessary, as much joint learning as possible', the Federal Government and the Federal States have, since the early 1970s, made DM 70 million available for pilot schemes and integration projects. There are, at the present time, some 40 schemes being carried out (BW, 1991b).

Often, individual care at the early stage, in kindergarten and primary school, is able to compensate for the occurrence of a handicap to such an extent that subsequent transfer to a special school is no longer required. This presumes, however, a thorough, special training for all teaching staff at normal schools and the motivation to take the particular problems of the individual child into consideration. The situation in the FRG is in many ways reminiscent of the development of integration in the UK. There are some innovatory integration projects in operation in certain parts of the country, and a lack of incentive and adherence to segregated special schooling in other areas. However, it is evident that the 'integration' rhetoric is being translated into practice in many länder. In the FRG there are many creative and innovative practices being developed through the theme of 'integration'. The aim, as in the UK, is to bring as many local education authorities or länder as possible into the new integrational practices.

CHAPTER 5

Greece

Greece is a small country which lies in the South Eastern part of Europe and has a population of approximately 10.25 million. About one third of the inhabitants live in Athens. The country is divided into 13 regions (periferies) and into 53 departments known as 'nomarhies'. In January 1 1981, Greece became a member of the EC.

The educational policy of the Greek Government rests on the basic assumption that 'education is a social good and something to which every citizen has a right" (Nicodemos, 1992). The State has an obligation to ensure this provision for every young person as an urgent priority, in every part of the country – with the same level and quality of preparation, the same visible and objective procedures, the same reliable and full provision of information about opportunities and conditions of study at all levels, about the specific needs of the economy, and about the situation in employment.

One of the basic objectives of the Greek educational policy is:

to seek out and develop the creative abilities and talents of all young people, to give these young people a systematic preparation for the difficult task of regenerating the country and ensuring its progress, in a responsible way, with critical understanding and, above all, as citizens equipped with adequate scientific and technical expertise (Nicodemos, 1992).'

The structure and operation of the Greek education system

Education is provided on three levels: primary education (nursery and primary schools), secondary education (gymnasia and lycea) and tertiary education which encompasses university-level education (AEI) and non-university education (TEI). Compulsory education lasts for nine years (six years at primary level and three years at secondary level).

Responsibility for the administration and operation of general, technical and vocational secondary schools lies with senior staff of the education directorates. Teachers and administrative employees work under the control of the directorates. At the same educational level, the responsibility for issuing guidance on teaching matters rests with the schools adviser whose duty it is to assess the performance of teachers and to arrange for their further training as well as to encourage educational research. The position of schools adviser was brought into being by law in 1982.

Special education in Greece

The provision of primary and secondary education for children with special educational needs is a multi-faceted new extension to education, as far as the Greek educational system is concerned. Until a few years ago, special education (EA) was provided only for a few children, mainly as inmates in homes run by various charitable foundations. In recent years, however, with the creation of the necessary legislative infrastructures in 1981, 1982 and 1983, there has been progress in the training of staff and the creation of a number of special schools.

One particular law, 1566/85, makes EA an integral part of general education, and the previously applicable separate legislation has been incorporated into the combined law on the structure and operation of primary and secondary education. The main elements affecting EA are:

1. *The creation of new branches* of skilled personnel (psychologists, speech therapists, social workers, physiotherapists, occupational therapists, assistants) who will be employed by the Ministry of Education to staff the EA units.
2. The creation by the Ministry of Education of the *Council for Special Education (SEA)*. This body will replace the old EA Council and has more representatives of the various services and social agencies.
3. The institution of measures and methods to achieve a closer coordination of the services responsible for *diagnosing* the problem of each child with special educational needs.
4. *The possibility of commencing* the provision of EA from the age of 3 years.
5. *The regulation of certain matters affecting the teaching staff* of special education units run by foundations governed by other ministries.

In October 1985 there were 167 special education units of all types and grades under the jurisdiction of the Ministry of Education. Of these, 151 were operated by the State and 16 were privately run. Ninety new special education units have been legislated for, over the whole country, and commenced operation from the 1985/86 school year. Ninety per cent of these are in the form of special classes in ordinary schools (known as school-incorporated special education).

The number of pupils with special educational needs who are following special education programmes in these units is 3,484. This number represents only 2 per cent of the total number of children in the 4–18 age group who, according to international statistics, have special educational needs, although this depends on the quality and therefore on the extent of the EA which a State wishes and is able to organize and offer. The more specialized and organized the EA provision is, the more individuals with special educational needs it can include.

Integration of Children with Special Needs in Rural Greece

Paul Bardis

Introduction

Integration is no longer an issue for the future – it is a present reality. It has become a new ecumenical movement for education. With increasing frequency, students with mild special needs are being educated in regular classrooms. Integration programmes, when well planned and implemented, can be of social and academic benefit for all students involved, both handicapped and non-handicapped.

We believe that, whenever possible, students should learn with their peers and that the regular classroom is the appropriate setting for the majority of those students who require special educational services during their school careers. Integration, however, is not a panacea; it is not appropriate for all impaired pupils; nor is it a simple procedure to initiate and maintain for those students who have the potential to profit from such an educational arrangement. To many special educators and parents, it is the preferred placement. In fact, parents often view the moment of integration as the first or most significant sign of success for their child with special needs. Integration is a welcome challenge and endeavours to provide information which will help regular educators be more effective participants in its exciting future.

Content and philosophy of integration

Ten professional educators using the term "integration" will generally mean ten different things by it. Integration, usually, refers to the process and product of interaction of children with special needs and normal children in educational settings and elsewhere on either a part- or full-time basis.

The term is also being used to connote a commonality of purpose and procedures in the education of students in primary and secondary schools, including those pupils labelled as mildly handicapped. For many of these students, it has been assumed that education should occur in special classes, isolated from other students and teachers in the school. Advocates of integration challenge this notion, pointing out that separate education can be inferior education and that special classes often result in education in which goals for students have been unnecessarily and arbitrarily limited. They also argue that placement in self-contained special classes tends to be permanent, since specialized curricula do not teach the content and study skills necessary for successful participation in the regular classroom.

Another more generic (and often preferred) term is, 'least restrictive environment'. This concept of least restrictive educational placement – that is, providing the maximum quantities and kind of integration – is being widely endorsed. Integration, although it is one very important keystone of education for impaired children, is not sufficient in itself. Comprehensive planning for these children must include consideration of programmes along a complete continuum so that every child will be able to attain his or her maximum educational, social and vocational potential. Integration cannot be expected to work without careful planning for each individual's needs.

The major beliefs which underlie placement of students with special needs in regular classrooms are:

- Students differ on a continuum of functional ability levels, so students referred by classroom teachers for special education services are more alike than different from their peers.
- Traditional special classes, with their separate curricula, tend to widen rather than narrow the differences between special education students and their regular class peers.
- Special classes introduce students into an artificial atmosphere, in which class size is smaller and expectations are often reduced. This makes later integration increasingly difficult.
- Special class services isolate students from their peers, either requiring attendance in other than one's neighbourhood school or placing students in a room with a less than desirable reputation among other students in the school.

- Special classes deprive regular students of opportunities to interact with students of lesser ability or skill. This allows prejudice to be fed by lack of contact.
- In integration programmes, classroom teachers are encouraged to learn new techniques and approaches for working with pupils with learning and behaviour problems, techniques which can be used with other students. This may help reduce the need for future referrals to special education.

There are many trends today lending support to the concept and actuality of integration. Among the factors pointing toward increased integration efforts in Greece are: increasing support for the rights of children, parental participation in educational issues, legislative and organizational support, and school changes including early identification, amplification and education.

Special education in Greece

Special education in Greece has a history of almost a century. The first special school was established in 1906; it was a private school for blind students. Another private school for deaf students was established in 1923. The first public special school was established in 1937. It was a school for mentally retarded children.

During the 1970s, special education increased rapidly. Tables 5.1 – 5.4 indicate the number of special education units, their distribution, the number of students in these units, and the number of special education teachers.

All these units belong to the Ministry of Education. There are also some other units (special schools and pre-vocational workshops) which belong to the Ministry of Health and Social Security; these units have not been included in Table 5.1. Most of the units indicated in Table 5.1 (approximately 150) are located in the major area of Athens, while the remaining units are found in the other parts of Greece.

Table 5.1 Special education units (1988/89)

Educational Units	Public	Private	Total
Kindergartens	25	2	27
Primary schools	113	10	123
Special classes (in regular schools)	285	—	285
High schools	11	—	11
Vocational schools	1	2	3
Total	435	14	449

Table 5.2 Distribution of special education units for each category of handicapped children (1988/89)

Category	Total	Kindergartens	Primary schools	High schools	Vocational schools
Blind	4	2	2	—	—
Hearing impaired	23	6	11	6	—
Physically handicapped	20	5	9	5	1
Mentally retarded	109	13	95	—	1
Socially maladjusted	8	1	6	—	1
Total	164	27	123	3	3

Table 5.3 Number of students age 4–18 receiving special services

Category	Primary	High School	Total
Blind	106	—	106
Hearing impaired	476	231	707
Physically handicapped	266	133	399
Mentally retarded	2.100	135	2.235
Socially maladjusted	81	49	130
Learning difficulties (special classes)	3.352	—	3.352
Total	6.381	548	6.929

*Note:*This number represents the academic year 1987/1988. Today the number of students is about 8,200.

Table 5.4 Special education teachers

Educational units	Public	Private	Total
Kindergartens	13	3	16
Primary schools	280	87	367
Special classes (in regular schools)	100	—	100
High schools	88	—	88
Vocational schools	20	32	52
Total	501	122	623

Note: The numbers in this table represent the academic year 1985/1986. Today the total number of special education teachers is about 1,000 (psychologists, social workers and other professionals are included).

There are also 3,500 students receiving special services in special education units which belong to the Ministry of Health and Social Security. This number has not been included in the above table.

The total number of pupils with special needs in Greece is estimated to be about 180,000 (10 per cent of the school age population).

School advisors for special education

For the coordination of the work in the field of special education, there are just 11 school advisors for all Greece; five of them have their offices in Athens. As can be appreciated, their work is very difficult because it is impossible for them to visit, even once a year, all special schools and classes in their vast educational areas.

Associations and organizations for special education

There are 80 associations, organizations, etc. of parents, educators and other professionals working for the improvement of special education in Greece and for the integration of students with special needs. Forty-five of them are in Athens and the other 35 in other Greek cities.

Referral, assessment and placement procedures in special education in Greece

Placement of a student in a special education unit is an eight-step process:

1. Regular teacher observes a problem.
2. Teacher initiates a referral.
3. Diagnostic team is formed.
4. The child is examined.
5. Placement decisions are made by the team.
6. Parents are informed by the team.
7. Parents agree with placement.
8. Placement in special education.

Step 1: For most students in special education, the process of placement begins with an observation by a regular classroom teacher. The teacher may observe that a student is not learning at a sufficient rate, or is engaging in socially disruptive or disturbing idiosyncratic behaviour.

Step 2: The teacher initiates a referral, by having made contact with the special education advisor (or with the primary education director of the district) and informing him or her about the problem.

Step 3: Upon receiving a referral, a school district will investigate the problem further. In the past, for this purpose, a diagnostic team of professionals was formed, after a Prefect's decision. There were 30 such prefectorial diagnostic teams, one for each prefecture. But now, each special school has its own psycho-diagnostic team comprising the special education teacher, a doctor, a social worker and a psychologist.

Step 4: The assessment team of the special school visits the regular school, talks with the classroom teacher and observes the child at work in the classroom.

The students who are severely or profoundly handicapped, or who have significant sensory, emotional or physical problems, should be seen by a number of professionals, representing a variety of disciplines. For this purpose, there are 20 medico-pedagogical centres in the major area of Athens and ten in other cities, belonging to the Ministry of Health and Social Security. In these centres, in order to determine whether a child is eligible for special education services, the assessment goes through the following steps:

a. tests of vision and learning;
b. medical history and medical examination;
c. social history (usually by a social worker);
d. educational history (including information on current academic performance);
e. administration of an individual intelligence test.

Step 5: All the above multiple sources of information for the assessment of the child are combined by the professionals, in order to determine appropriate placement and educational programmes for the student.

There are two necessary decisions which must be made sequentially: first it must be determined whether the student is eligible for special education services. This decision most often focuses on diagnostic information and involves determination of the special education category, under which the student will be treated. If the student is eligible for services, the second decision relates to placement in a special education programme.

Step 6: After the diagnosis and the decisions have been made, the professionals (usually the social worker) present the data to the parents and ask their permission for their child's placement.

Step 7: No placement can be done without obtaining parent's permission.

Step 8: Once parental permission has been obtained, the child is placed in the appropriate special education category, under which the student will be treated.

Integration of children with special needs in rural Greece

In most Greek villages there are no special education units of any kind for handicapped children. As we mentioned previously, in the major area of Athens there are 150 special education units and 300 in other cities and small towns. In Karditsa, for example, there are four units: 1 kindergarten, 1 primary school and 2 classes. In the central part of the Greek mainland there are about 50 special education units.

To manage integration in rural Greece (and all over Greece), three types of special education units are being used: a) special school; b) special class; and c) pre-vocational workshop.

a. Special school

Special education occurs within an ordinary school. The students who attend a special school have a chronological age from 5 to 11 and they are sensorily and physically handicapped, mentally retarded, socially maladjusted or students with learning difficulties and behaviour problems.

The students of the special school are classified under five levels, according to their IQ:

i)   Pre-school level;
ii) Lower level (IQ: 25–35);
iii) Middle level (IQ: 35–45);
iv) High level (IQ: 45–65);
v)   Higher level (IQ: 65–75).

All students in the special school are integrated with regular students, playing together in the school yard during the breaks. The students of the high and higher levels leave the self-contained classroom to join normal children in a regular classroom for those non-academic subjects in which the staff feel he or she can successfully participate. This partial and non-academic integration may include physical education, home economics, arts and crafts, music, traffic education, and field trips.

b. Special class

The special class is a new institution in the field of special education. Its basic aim is the educational and social integration of students with special needs. In a special class, students (no more than 15) include those with learning difficulties, behaviour problems, immigrant parents, social disadvantages and with borderline intelligence (IQ: 70–85). With a special class which belongs to a regular school, we manage a full or complete integration, because the children with special needs attend regular classes. However, the special child receives additional specific services in the special class (about three to six hours per week), programmed to his or her special needs.

The special class is a very positive institution for the integration of children with special needs and it has been accepted by teachers, parents and students. There are 285 such special classes all over Greece; 87 of them are found in the major area of Athens and the remainder in other cities and small towns. In the central part of the Greek mainland (with a population of about 921,000 inhabitants) there are 41 special classes.

c. Pre-vocational workshop

Unfortunately, there are no such workshops in rural Greece, but there are about 25 Vocational Schools and Pre-vocational Workshops in Athens and in some other big cities, operating in institutions and hospitals and belonging to the Ministries of Work and Social Security. Handicapped students, with an age of 15 and above, attend these schools for social and vocational mainstreaming. But these 25 schools and workshops are not enough to cover the vocational needs of all handicapped students in Greece.

As we mentioned earlier, the total number of children with special needs is estimated to be 180,000. Most of them, about 90 per cent, are children with mild handicaps and sensory impairments. All of them attend regular classes. However, this is not to say that these children are completely integrated, because they do not receive any additional specific services. The sensorily impaired children especially who daily face many difficulties in the normal class, after two or three years (it depends upon their difficulties) abandon regular school without any social mainstreaming.

With regard to the Thessalian University (in Volos), where I teach special education, within the framework of my courses ('Introduction to Special

Education I and II'), I organize visits to different special education units in the district. This way, I sensitize my students and I introduce them to integration, by preparing them to accept 'special needs' children to their regular classes in the future as pre-school and primary education teachers.

A major aspiration of the Greek Ministry of Education is to reinforce integration as much as possible, by planning to increase the number of special education units, especially the number of special classes, the number of special advisors and the specific services for children with special needs.

Difficulties in managing integration in rural Greece

We face many problems in managing integration in Greece, especially in rural areas; the most important of them are given below.

1. Social prejudice and ignorance: there is no sensitization or education of society for the problems and the special needs of impaired children. Parents of normal children do not want special schools and special classes in their neighbourhood or in the ordinary schools. Because of ignorance, in many cases the children with special needs are seen as a problem for charitable institutions. The results of this situation are unsuitable buildings for special schools, many children with different handicaps in the same class, lack of audio-visual materials, lack of experience in the education of children with special needs, etc.

2. Many regular teachers and the administration are not prepared to meet the needs of handicapped children. Consequently, such children are removed from their regular classroom and placed in a segregated programme.

3. The attitude of regular teachers towards special teachers and special children is generally very negative. They are often not cooperative and they initiate referrals of children with very mild handicaps, who could stay in the regular class. Many regular classroom teachers do not want impaired children in their classes and are hesitant to teach them the skills and knowledge necessary for adult functioning in our society.

4. There is no periodic review procedure. For many students, placement in special education has been permanent, with little or no opportunity to return to complete participation in the regular education programme.

5. Regular educators express concern that returning the exceptional child to the regular classroom will somehow dilute educational programmes for non-handicapped children. But the 'normal' child will profit from learning and working with his or her handicapped peers, especially when the regular teacher: a) uses procedures that will accommodate the learning and social needs of each individual child; b) develops attitudes of acceptance for the

child with special needs; and c) receives competent support of specialists and aids as required.

6. There are only 11 school advisors for special education in all Greece; five of them have their offices in Athens. It is impossible for them to coordinate the work of integration in their vast educational areas.

7. The number of special teachers is not sufficient to cover the needs of special education. So, in many cases, handicapped children are found in regular classrooms with teachers who do not want them or who do not know how to teach children with special needs.

8. The total number of students with special needs is estimated to be about 180,000. But only 5 per cent of them are receiving special services. In Thessaly (the prefectures of Volos, Larisa, Trikala and Karditsa in the central part of the Greek mainland, with a population of 700,000 inhabitants) only 130 students with special needs are receiving special services.

9. Parents of children with special needs are often not cooperative and they do not want to enrol their children in special school and classes because they do not accept their child's problem. Beyond that, they demand that special teachers teach their children reading, writing, arithmetic, etc.

10. Special classes do not have a diagnostic team. So, the information from parents, regular teachers, etc. is not sufficient to make educational progress with students.

11. The diagnostic team of a special school visits a regular school, whenever a regular teacher initiates a referral. They do this during working hours so, often, the special school remains without its scientific staff, especially in difficult and distant geographical areas.

12. After students reach 17 years of age, the students with special needs leave special school or special class and return to their homes, without any mainstreaming, either social or vocational.

13. Special schools are not economically independent. They depend on the budget of regular schools, so it is difficult for them to meet their operational costs.

14. The EC covers 55 per cent of the expenses of vocational training programmes for children with special needs but, so far, there are no such vocational schools in rural Greece.

How to improve integration in rural Greece

1. Education is entering a new era, in which regular and special educators are expected to pool their talents and work together to educate students. This is an exciting prospect. Developments in this direction will be of substantial

benefit to both students and teachers. No one, regular or special teacher, should do the job alone. All must continue to learn to work together.

2. The goals of an integration programme should remain child-oriented and should include the development of effective communication, academic and vocational achievement, independence, and social sufficiency.

3. Integrated education should be pursued with a commitment and competence that will help to break education's moratorium on individual learning.

4. In-service training of regular teachers in special education is of great importance.

5. There is a need for more special teachers in rural areas.

6. We need more special school advisors. We cannot talk about integration, when we have only 10 advisors in all Greece!

7. We need more special classes in small towns and villages for complete academic integration of children with mild handicaps. In these classes children will receive some additional specific services, geared to their special needs.

8. We need periodic review procedures for the students in special schools, so that their placement will not be permanent. Students should have the opportunity to return to regular schools, according to their progress.

9. There is a need for the development of programmes for the improvement of audio-visual materials, teaching methods, etc. and of information and presentation through the mass media, in order to face the problem of social prejudice.

10. The establishment of special education departments at peripheral universities is necessary.

11. There is a need for the establishment of counselling centres, one for each prefecture. This team of professionals, representing a variety of disciplines (special educator, social worker, psychologist, child psychiatrist, speech therapist, physiotherapist) will be responsible for informing parents, teachers and the public (through TV, radio, papers, etc.), for early diagnosis of handicapped children by visiting regular schools, and for the placement of children with special needs.

12. There must be an increase of kindergartens for an early confrontation of problems in childhood.

13. There is a need for the development of specialized medico-pedagogical centres at the peripheral and university hospitals.

14. Special education should be compulsory and should begin as soon as possible after the early diagnosis.

15. Special classes should have the support of specialized professionals for a correct assessment of children.

16. The fulfilment of all the above requires more money either from the state budget or from the EC.

17. Regarding sensorily impaired children, many of them, as we stated earlier, are placed in regular classrooms. The above suggestions are provided to help regular teachers to deal effectively with these students.

In conclusion, integration is no longer an issue for the future – it is a present reality. It is a welcome challenge for all of us. We must work very hard and all together, in order to help students with special needs to find a place in regular education and later in our society.

CHAPTER 6

Ireland

Ireland (Eire) is a small island to the West of the European land mass. It is a country divided into the Republic of Ireland and Northern Ireland (which is governed within the United Kingdom). Ireland, in total, has a population of approximately 5 million; 3.5 million live in the Republic of Ireland. Gaelic and English are the official languages in Ireland. Compulsory schooling is for nine years, from 6–15 years of age.

Since 1922 Ireland has been known as the Republic of Ireland and is made up of 26 counties. The education system is run by the Minister for Education who is a member of the Irish Government and responsible to the National Parliament. The education system is denominational and this must be seen against the background of historical developments and constitutional provisions. In the 1937 Constitution, the State acknowledged that the family was the primary educator of the child, and parents were free to choose to educate their children at home, in private schools or in state recognized or established schools. The State's constitutional duty was to provide for free first-level education and to supplement and aid private and corporate initiatives when the public good required it. This was related to the system established under Britain in the late nineteenth century, which encouraged the development of a primary school system based on voluntary local initiatives and under local control and management. The State did not undertake to provide schools but would aid their provision in response to local initiatives. These local initiatives were mostly taken by the church and religious denominations with the result that the system, in practice, became a denominational one.

Secondary schools are privately owned and managed institutions which must be recognized by the Department of Education and subject to its regulations. Vocational schools are administered by vocational education committees which mainly consist of local authority members. Comprehensive and community schools are administered by Boards of Management. Comprehensive schools are managed by Boards comprising representation from the diocesan religious authority, the vocational education committee of the area and the Minister for Education. Community schools are managed by representatives of local interests, ie, the local vocational education committee, the religious communities, the parents and the teachers. About 95 per cent of secondary schools participate in a scheme of free education for young people, regardless of family circumstances. Secondary schools receive considerable financial assistance from the Department of Education, almost full payment of teachers salaries and allowances, and approved buildings and equipment. There are capitation grants for each eligible pupil and grants for pupils' fees, to schools participating in the free education scheme. Almost the total cost of vocational education is met by the Department of Education, with the remainder provided by the Vocational Education Committees.

Comprehensive and community schools are financed entirely by the State through the Department of Education. In the higher education sector, the pattern is very much the same. The State covers a considerable part of the budgets of universities and other higher education institutions and reserves for itself the right to participate in the planning and budget management of higher education.

The Irish School Attendance Act of 1926 and subsequent amendment require that children attend school between the ages of 6 and 15. However, children may enter national school at the age of 4, and almost half do at present; the average age for beginning school is 5. The majority of pupils transfer to second-level schooling at 12 years of age.

Pre-school education

There is no national system of pre-schools or nurseries in Ireland; however there are more than half of 4-year-olds and almost 100 per cent of 5 year olds enrolled in infant classes in primary schools.

The curriculum followed during the two years of pre-compulsory schooling is part of an integrated programme extended over the eight years of first-level schooling. The pre-school educational services which do exist have developed mainly on a voluntary private basis. Provision of this kind is not normally financed by the Department of Education, as it is not part of the formal education system. Parents normally pay fees except for pre-school provision for travellers' children. There are some 40 nursery schools for travellers children, run by local voluntary associations which are given grants by the Department of Education towards tuition and transport costs. It is usual for day care services for children to be provided by voluntary organizations or approved individuals with financial support from the Department of Health, especially for the children of disadvantaged families or in areas of social disadvantage. The Department of Health organizes, through the area Health Boards, substantial services for children with disabilities before they reach the compulsory school age of 6 years. Therefore children with serious handicaps have access to pre-school education. Children with visual or hearing impairment are supported by peripatetic teaching services.

Primary schooling

First-level education in Ireland covers a period of eight years. National schools are state-aided schools but they are not state schools. The majority of schools are organized on a denominational basis, although in recent years parents have succeeded in establishing six new national schools on a multi-denominational basis. In response to local demand, national schools have been established in which pupils are educated through the medium of the Irish language or Gaelic.

The number of national schools in Ireland is around 3,400, catering for some 561,000 pupils. The total number of national school teachers is about 21,200. The first-level pupil:teacher ratio is approximately 27:1 (Department of Education, 1989).

Special education

In the past in Ireland, there were schools for children with visual and hearing impairment and one institution in Dublin for people with a 'mental handicap'. It wasn't until the 1950s that parents, professionals, religious orders and others created voluntary associations which established their own national schools for children with a 'mental handicap'. The ordinary national school was not able to accept these children, so special schools were established in most of the 26 counties and in some cases special classes were established in schools in a number of large towns. Pupils in both special schools and classes were allowed free transport.

In the 1960s there grew an awareness of the need for additional help and support in basic subjects, especially reading in the ordinary school for a large number of children. 'Remedial education' was established to provide this help and support by the provision of additional specialized teaching on an individual or small group basis. Pupils who were having difficulty with reading, and to a lesser extent with mathematics, were withdrawn from normal classes to receive special help from a remedial teacher for 30–40 minutes daily.

One of the main aims of the Curaclam na Bunscoile (Department of Education, 1971) was to respond to the individual needs of all pupils. Schools began developing programmes of instruction to achieve this aim and the needs of pupils with moderate school learning difficulties were highlighted. There was a demand from schools for remedial teachers, and during the 1970s and early 1980s the number of full-time remedial teachers expanded to the present level of approximately 800 (Department of Education, 1989).

Because Ireland has no law on integration, and still has a parallel system of special education run by the Department of Health and the Department of Education, the system of remedial education is important to support pupils with learning difficulties in schools. However, the precise form the organization of such teaching adopts depends upon the decision of head-teachers. The Department of Education's guidelines on 'Remedial Education' stipulates that the school principal, in consultation with the staff should decide on:

- an overall programme which is aimed at meeting the needs of all the pupils in the school;
- a policy for remedial education as part of the overall school programme;
- the allocation of teaching personnel, time and material resources;
- forms of communication within the school, between the school and the home, between the school and post-primary schools and other relevant agencies;
- means of monitoring the progress of special help programmes as part of a general evaluation of the work of the school;
- the precise contribution which each member of staff is to make to the attainment of the aims of the remedial programme in the school.

The remedial teacher is the person in the school who is responsible for keeping records for children who are receiving special help. The main activities of the remedial teacher are set out as follows:

- to advise on school policy and plans on language, reading and mathematics;
- to advise colleagues on the special needs of individual children;
- to advise colleagues on diagnosis and special help programmes;
- to coordinate special help programmes throughout the school;
- to plan and monitor prevention programmes;
- to advise the principal and colleagues on the availability, suitability and the use of equipment for children with special needs;
- to prepare teaching materials for use throughout the school;

- to develop resource centres for language, reading and mathematics;
- to assist in the development of a system of record-keeping for children with special needs;
- to liaise with parents and advise them on their role in a remedial programme;
- to communicate with other professionals and agencies both inside and outside the school who are involved with individual children.

The remedial teacher is accepted as a professional with a wide range of skills. She or he is expected to have expertise in the diagnosis and remediation of learning difficulties, and to make a contribution to the general school programme planning in reading, language and maths at all levels. The remedial teacher is seen as an adviser and a resource teacher and to be competent in organization, administration and record keeping. It is also expected that the remedial teacher will be capable of a high level of interpersonal skills, to fulfil the role of professional negotiator with parents and colleagues. Special schools in Ireland were originally established as national schools, and it is anachronistic that they are still run under this banner, as they provide for children and young people up to the age of 18 years. Within the special school there is a division drawn between a junior and a senior section. Numbers of pupils in special schools have grown since the 1950s: in 1957 there were 1,500 pupils in special classes and schools, in 1980 there were 11,000 (McGee, 1990), and today that number remains relatively stable at 11,500 (see Table 6.1).

We can see from this table that the categorization of pupils with special needs in Ireland is still used to define pupils with handicaps, disabilities, learning difficulties and social disadvantage. We also see that there are four special schools for 'travellers' children and 73 special classes for travellers in ordinary schools. This is the largest group of pupils in special classes with the exception of classes for mildly mentally handicapped. We also see the use of the terms 'mildly' and 'moderately mentally handicapped'. The Report of the Commission on Mental Handicap (Department of Health, 1965) in Ireland recommend the use of the term 'mental handicap' on three levels, ie, mild, moderate and severe, which relates to intelligence quotients with an upper limit of 70, 50 and 35 respectively. We will now look in more detail at the provision for children with different special needs in Ireland.

Children with mild handicap

We may observe in Table 6.1 that there are a large number of pupils considered to be mildly mentally handicapped: 3,508 in special schools and 1,649 in special classes, which is 45 per cent of the total number of pupils

Table 6.1 Special schools and special classes, 1990/91

	Number of schools	Number of classes	Total boys	Total girls	Total enrolment
SPECIAL SCHOOLS					
1 Schools for mildly mentally handicapped	32	245	2,101	1,407	3,508
2 Schools for moderately mentally handicapped	33	216	1,332	941	2,273
3 Schools for young offenders and disadvantaged	10	38	267	92	359
4 Schools for emotionally disturbed	14	53	349	88	437
5 Hospital schools for physically handicapped	6	9	73	50	123
6 Schools for physically handicapped	7	41	257	207	464
7 Schools for hearing impaired	5	94	287	294	581
8 Schools for travellers	4	15	122	87	209
9 Schools for multiply handicapped	2	8	35	11	46
10 Schools for blind/partially sighted	2	14	49	78	127
11 Schools for children with reading disability	2	11	116	26	142
Total	117	744	4,988	3,281	8,269
SPECIAL CLASSES					
1 Schools for mildly mentally handicapped	112	158	989	660	1,649
2 Schools for moderately mentally handicapped	3	4	29	17	46
3 Classes for hearing impaired	3	4	17	4	21
4 Classes for language impaired	4	7	42	15	57
5 Classes for travellers	73	118	692	770	1,462
Total	195	291	1,769	1,466	3,235
Total for special schools and special classes					11,504

Source: Department of Education, 1992

in special classes and schools. Most of these pupils have spent their earlier school career in the ordinary classes of national schools and a significant number enter special schools and classes at 12 years of age at secondary school transfer. Special schools as a whole are generally better resourced than special classes (McGee, 1990). The reason is that voluntary associations or religious orders can raise extra funds to employ professionals other than teachers and support services that are not available to other special schools or to special classes. Schools with a special class operate a pupil:teacher ratio of 16:1, which is the official ratio for special schools and classes. However, in special classes in large schools there is often a wide age span of pupils, and because the special class is self-contained, it is not fully integrated into the ordinary school life.

Children between the ages of 4 and 18 are educated in schools for pupils with mild mental handicap. Entry to these schools is approved only after the deliberation of a full psychological assessment and with parental consent. In addition to the special schools, 158 special classes attached to ordinary schools are now recognized. Such classes have a maximum pupil:teacher ratio of 16:1 and transport to and from school is provided free of charge.

Children with moderate mental handicap

There are 33 schools and three classes for pupils with moderate mental handicap. There are 2,319 pupils categorized in this way, accounting for 20 per cent of all pupils in special schools and classes (see Table 6.1). Numerically, therefore, children with mild and moderate mental handicap form the largest single category of all forms of handicap. The development of education for this group of children derives principally from recommendations in the Report of the Commission of Inquiry on Mental Handicap, 1965. The Commission gave great consideration to the part which day and residential special schools and special classes should play in the provision of education for the mildly mentally handicapped. Having considered the merits of the arguments for and against the segregation of handicapped pupils, the Commission decided in favour of special schools. In the course of time, since this decision was made, departmental policy tended to favour special classes rather than special schools, and recent growth in provision has reflected this tendency.

Children with severe and profound handicap

There are 17 classes attached to special schools, which provide appropriate education and training for children with severe and profound mental handicap. These classes are under the responsibility of the Department of Health. At present, teachers who are paid and supervised by the Department of Education are available on a pilot basis for approximately 200 pupils in this category.

Children with emotional disturbance

There are 14 schools for children with emotional disturbance. The schools are situated mainly in the Dublin area and are associated with child guidance clinics. Children in these schools also receive psychiatric treatment. There are 437 pupils receiving education in this category. Some of these schools operate on a short-term basis, the aim of which is to return pupils to the ordinary school within one or two years; others provide long-term education for pupils with more permanent or long-term problems.

Children with physical handicap

There are seven schools in total for pupils with physical disability or handicap. Four of these schools are in the Dublin area, the others are in Cork, Limerick and Bray. A total of 464 pupils attend these schools. However, there are also a large number of children with physical handicaps already attending ordinary national schools, although we have no precise figures. Yet because the seven special schools are in large urban areas, it is often the case that these pupils will also be found in the local school or the nearest special school in more rural areas.

Children with visual impairment

The needs of pupils with visual impairment are met through two special schools in Dublin, one in Merrion and the other in Drumcondra. One school is for junior children aged 4–16 years, while the other is for boys aged 8–12 years, who transfer to a community school on the same campus where special provision has been organized. Outside the Dublin area, pupils' needs are met in the local school with the support of a visiting teacher service.

Children with hearing impairment

Until recently, services for children with hearing impairment were centralized in three special schools in Dublin. Following the report of a special committee in 1972, a Visiting Teacher Service was established to provide teaching and counselling for children and their families throughout the country. The service focuses on pre-school hearing impaired children, and gives advice and support to children who are placed in ordinary schools. In recent years special schools were established beyond Dublin, in Cork and Limerick. More recently parents have demanded that a number of special units be established in ordinary schools to cater for the needs of children with hearing impairment. Four of these units are now in operation. There are approximately 600 pupils being taught in special schools and classes at present. It is estimated that there are more than twice that number enrolled in ordinary schools (Department of Education, 1988).

Children with language disorders and specific reading disabilities

There are special facilities attached to three ordinary schools in Dublin for children with language impairment, one of which is temporary. There are also three special schools for children with specific reading disabilities, two in Dublin and one in Cork. These schools are provided for children with considerable difficulties in reading and are required to return pupils to the ordinary school within two years. The units for children with language impairment are provided for small groups of children with a serious language disorder. Each unit or class is staffed by a specialist teacher and a speech therapist employed by the Regional Health Board. The teacher is a member of the ordinary school staff.

A report from the Primary Education Review Body, 1990 has resulted in the establishment of a Special Committee to report on the educational provisions for children with special needs. This Committee will be investigating further a number of issues of concern to the Department of Education in Ireland, as follows:

- The integration of pupils with special needs into the general education system.
- The appointment of additional care personnel.
- The coordination of services for handicapped children.
- The provision of an appropriate visiting teacher service and home tuition for all handicapped children.
- The development of remedial education.
- The provision of schooling for pupils with special needs at post-primary level.
- The methods of identification of pupils with special learning needs.
- The clarification and coordination of different government departments in the role of special needs.

- The guidance and information needed for parents, teachers and school authorities on the services available.
- The use of modern technology in the education of children with special needs.
- The provision of curricular guidelines.
- The development of pre-service and in-service training of teachers for pupils with special needs.
- The review of class size.
- The development of a network of ancillary and professional services.
- The necessity of a minimum level of provision for children with particular handicaps.
- The establishment of an independent advisory service for parents on school placement.
- The possible provision of an assessment statement for each child with special needs in order to determine the appropriate level of provision needed in each case.

It appears now, since the inception of this Committee, that there will be a detailed analysis of the multiple issues related to handicapped children undertaken by a wide range of persons with special knowledge and expertise. McGee (1992) reports that alongside the Committee's work is the proposal that there should be an education act, and the first stage in that process, the publication of a Green Paper, is awaiting Governmental approval at present.

This is a welcome procedure which may lead the way to a much-needed review of present provision and procedures for special needs pupils. However, there have been a number of significant developments in the field of primary education since the Commission of Inquiry on Mental Handicap reported in 1965. The introduction of the new curriculum for primary schools in 1971 made the ordinary primary school a much more acceptable place for pupils with special needs. The official policy of the Department of Education is now one of integration of children with handicaps, where this is possible, while retaining the option of segregation when necessary. The Minister for Education in common with other ministers for Education in the European Community has contributed to a declaration to pursue a policy of integration. In 1987 at the Council of the European Communities the Irish Minister for Education, alongside her EC colleagues, reaffirmed the importance of achieving the maximum possible integration of handicapped children into ordinary schools (Council of the EC, 1987). There are however, considerable financial implications attached to such a policy in Ireland, in view of the present situation for pupils with special needs which only partially meets their needs within an educational context.

A major review is currently under way in the Department of Health of services for persons with a mental handicap. The review suggests that children at present considered to have a 'mild mental handicap' will in future be considered to be an educational concern related more to learning disability which will come under the aegis of the Department of Education. This move is to be welcomed as both a major change in perception and attitude to pupils who are experiencing school failure without any obvious reason and who form the major group of pupils with special needs within the school system. Yet the major contrast in Ireland to other EC countries is the lack of legislation to form the foundation for the educational rights of handicapped and disadvantaged children in society. It will require a major commission on the whole field of special needs provision and a wider raising of awareness, especially among politicians in the new government, to push the situation into the twenty-first century, to avoid lagging behind the initiatives and practices of EC countries like Spain who have recently attained membership.

In order to demonstrate to member states in the EC that practices in Ireland are reflecting a positive move towards integration, there needs to be a commitment to substantial and much needed legislation in this area.

CHAPTER 7

Italy

Italy is a large country in the South of Europe with a population of approximately 57 million. It is officially known as the Italian Republic and the official language is Italian. Italy's education system is a uni-dimensional single education framework for all children and there are nine years of compulsory schooling. Only 1.8 per cent of school children are considered 'handicapped' or to have special educational needs in Italy. Within this group the main categories identified are shown in Table 7.1.

The biggest group of 'handicapped' children are those categorized as 'mentally retarded'. Children with mild or moderate learning difficulties are not identified within this category and the children with 'mental retar-dation or learning difficulties' are normally taught in the ordinary school with the help of a support teacher. There are 36,000 (1988) support teachers in ordinary schools with the ratio of 1:2.7 handicapped pupils, and the maximum number of pupils per class is set at 25. If there are more than 25 pupils in one class, a second class is established. If there is a 'handicapped' pupil in the class, maximum numbers are set at 20, and only one 'handicapped' pupil is recommended per class.

Almost one quarter of classes in Italy have 'handicapped' pupils and these

Table 7.1 Percentage of children with special needs, by 'handicap'

	% of all pupils	% of all handicapped pupils
Visually impaired	0.04	2
Hearing impaired	0.11	6
Physically disabled	0.31	17
Mentally retarded	1.00	56
Emotionally disturbed	0.34	19
Total	1.80	100

Source: Ease, 1990

pupils are therefore in classes of 20 or less. They have a full-time teacher and a support teacher for, on average, a further ten hours. Support teachers work in the mainstream classroom and may also make use of a resource room for individual pupils or groups. Grouping of handicapped pupils rarely occurs. All Italian parents are very much in favour of inclusion or the integration of all pupils into mainstream schools. Because of this situation which emphasizes the special resources in mainstream schools, we need to consider the ordinary education system in Italy.

The educational system in Italy

In Italy the whole of primary, secondary and higher education is managed centrally by the Minister of Public Instruction (MPI). This does not mean to say that Italian education is placed entirely in the hands of the State: alongside the network of state schools, there is an important network of public schools which are not dependent on the State (governed, for example, by towns and communities) and also private schools. For the school year 1989/90, the percentage of pupils enrolled in private schools was 8 per cent at primary level, 4.5 per cent in the first stage of secondary level and 9.1 per cent in the second stage of secondary level. All schools, whether dependent on the State or not, whether public or private, conform to the national laws as well as the decrees and rules brought in by the MPI.

Schools not dependent on the State, as well as private schools which follow programmes of study finalized by the State and which offer sufficient guarantees as regards the educational curriculum, can be recognized by the State, with all the consequences that this implies for the legal status of students, the validation of study programmes, etc.

With reforms pending in public administration, currently, the main bodies responsible for the organization of education are the nine general management units which cover the following areas: primary; secondary (first level); secondary (second level): classical and scientific, and technical education; professional training; cultural exchanges; personnel and administration; buildings and equipment. Specific sectors such as sport and physical education, arts education and boarding schools are placed under the control of 3 inspectorates.

Another important body at ministerial level is the 'Office of Study and Planning' (Ufficio Studie Programmazione). It is the national body responsible for coordinating research initiatives, further education of students and experimentation. Pre-primary education is governed by its own department, the pre-primary school service.

The Minister for Public Instruction is not only the head of the central administration of education, but also the director of the National Council of Public Instruction, which is the supreme consultative body for all matters concerning education below the higher level. It is the duty of the Council to evaluate the activities and services of a school and to finalize the teaching programmes. The Minister of Public Instruction must submit to the Council for approval all propositions regarding legislative and administrative matters of importance. On a practical level, the central power of the MPI is exercised by delegations and ministerial branches at both regional and provincial levels. For each of the 20 regions of Italy, there is a Regional Superintendent nominated by the Minister. The Superintendent's powers are as follows:

- organization and administration of the selection procedures of teaching staff for positions in secondary education (concorsi);
- coordination between central administration and regional and local bodies.

On the whole, it can be said that the influence of the central authority over the regional powers remains problematic. All the same, there is evidence of a tendency in regional authorities towards increasing influence, particularly with regard to the establishment of regional priorities in teaching.

At a provincial level, the Minister is represented by provincial governors of education who are more or less the local branch representatives of central administration. The provincial governors of education and their services are of considerable importance. The principal task is to ensure the enforcement of laws and regulations that apply to primary and secondary educational establishments, both private and public. The heads and teachers in primary and secondary schools are directly responsible to the provincial governors of education.

The provincial governors of education are obliged to consult, although not necessarily to take up the advice of, the provincial School Councils which are made up of representatives of teachers and parents as well as provincial and local authorities, regarding teaching problems in the province in question.

In 1974 a law required that regional governments should allow for school districts with their own administrative autonomy and to gradually raise money towards this end. The district would be made up of rural and urban regions with common social and economic characteristics.

Pre-school education

The evolution of pre-school education in Italy has been influenced in the main by legislation passed in 1968, which established the current system of

State nurseries for children between the ages and of 3 and 5. These State nurseries accommodate more than 47 per cent of children of this age. The remainder of this population is under the supervision of the municipal, public nurseries, private, non-religious institutions and private religious institutions. Of children between 3 and 5 years old, 90.5 per cent (1,650,000) go to a nursery school.

Children between the ages of 3 and 5 are not obliged to attend pre-school establishments. Private establishments are, on the whole, fee-paying, whilst public establishments are free of charge. The 1968 Act, mentioned above, clearly stipulates that pre-school education should not consist of education in the strict sense of the word. The aim of the nursery school is to help children in their personal development and to prepare them for going to school when it is compulsory at 6 years. It is also aimed at complementing the educational efforts of the parents in order to avoid any imbalance or social maladjustment. In practice, these are the same rules which apply to all the establishments, be they in the public or private sector.

Since the 1968 legislation was adopted, special efforts have been made to establish pre-primary schools in the parts of the country where there are specific needs. These efforts have enabled the attendance figures to increase quite considerably.

It is the Minister for Public Instruction who has general responsibility for the pre-school establishments, although the management of nursery school is, in fact, entrusted to the local authorities for educational matters.

Compulsory education

In Italy, compulsory education commences at 6 years and continues to 14 years of age, consisting of five years of primary school and three years of secondary school, which is cycle one of secondary education. The Government has proposed the introduction of compulsory education for a longer period, from 8 to 10 years, that is, up to the age of 16. In 1990, 87 per cent of students in middle school went onto the higher level of secondary education.

Compulsory education is governed by national laws and regulations which apply throughout the country, that is to say, in both public and private establishments. In public schools, compulsory education is free of charge.

Primary education

Italian children spend their first five years of compulsory education in primary schools (scuola elementare). This five-year period is divided into two cycles, one of two years, and one of three years, which culminate in an official examination. The primary school certificate is required in order to pass into secondary education.

Primary education in Italy is available both in public and private schools. There are, however, very few private schools. The aims and programmes of teaching in the primary schools are defined and approved at national level. The very traditional programmes for the first two years (reading, writing and arithmetic) gradually change over the three year period with the introduction of such subjects as religious instruction (optional), civics, history, geography, arithmetic, Italian language, art, singing, craft and physical education. New programmes, recently approved by Parliament, have come into being since the school year 1990/91. Although it can be said that there have not been any striking reforms in the primary education field in Italy for some years, it should be pointed out that the pupil education system has been modified quite considerably.

In order to go through to the higher class, pupils are no longer chosen according to their average mark. Their ability and motivation are assessed on the basis of observation by the teacher throughout their school education and are the subject of written reports which take the form of a personal file (scheda), with the objective of compiling a complete profile on the personal attitudes of the pupil.

The average number of hours of class teaching in Italian primary schools is 24 a week, made up of four lessons a day, from Monday to Saturday. In some schools, at their request, extra time for lessons have been introduced on an experimental basis. This has enabled new subjects and activities to be introduced, such as linguistic expression, musical, artistic and technological activities, etc.

During the course of the school year 1989/90, the 28,786 primary schools in Italy had 2,892,740 pupils enrolled and there were 272,900 teachers in public schools in Italy.

Secondary education

The three final years of obligatory schooling (from 11 to 14 years) take place in middle schools (scuola media). These schools offer all subjects and give to all pupils of the age range concerned, whatever their background and social status, a free traditional education. Their aim is as much to prepare for adulthood and citizenship as to prepare pupils for further study. A very high percentage of students attend this type of school – 99.4 per cent during the course of the school year in 1989/90.

There are 30 hours of obligatory lessons a week: religion, Italian, history, civics, geography, maths, observation science, natural science, a foreign language, art and physical education. The Act of June 1977 has introduced technical and musical education as compulsory; at the same time, Latin has ceased to be a subject in itself. The Act is also concerned with the extension of interdisciplinary activities which can become a complement to the official teaching in the different subjects defined in the programme. In addition, the law insists that teachers offer to the pupil subjects such as mathematics, chemistry, physics and natural sciences, using methods which enable the pupil to understand the logical relationship between seemingly different elements of scientific knowledge.

As for evaluation, a new regulation came into being in 1977 which suppressed the traditional marking system based on points (1 to 10) given by each teacher as well as the remedial examinations. In addition, the former individual school file (pagella) has been replaced by the personal file (scheda personale) which the class teachers write and keep regularly up to date, together with pupils. This personal file gives a written account of attitudes, attendances, behaviour and the level attained by each pupil. On the basis of the remarks noted here, the class teachers prepare every three or four months an analytical report for each subject and an educational, all-round evaluation of the general level attained by the pupil. The teachers explain these reports to the parents who also receive a copy. The evaluation of the pupil's work as well as the final report are the basis of a certificate declaring the compulsory period of education has been completed. This certificate is attached to the personal file of each pupil and affirms that he or she has finished compulsory schooling.

At the end of the third year, the pupils have to pass the end-of-middle-school examination. This examination is organized by the teachers and by an outside inspector. For the pupils who pass this examination, advice and suggestions regarding the pursuance of further study are attached to the certificate.

During the school year 1989/90, the 10,057 middle schools had 2,284,800 pupils on roll, and of the 787,398 pupils who left secondary school after the first cycle, 631,000 passed onto the second cycle.

Integration of pupils with special educational needs

The Italian legislation has guaranteed, since 1977, the integration of hand-icapped pupils into ordinary schools in connection with obligatory school-ing, where there must be assurances of the necessary specialized support and services for students' education. In 1987 the Constitutional Court extended the same guarantee to the secondary high schools.

The basic principles of integration and the definition of 'handicapped'

The national position on integration has only been defined for a few years, in fact it was only a few years ago that legislation gave the same rights to disabled pupils as able-bodied pupils. Article 38 of the Constitution gives full rights to the handicapped but as yet there is no State law to define the term 'handicapped'. The Constitutional Court made a ruling concerning the enrolment and attendance of handicapped children up to second grade in high (secondary) school in 1987. This represented a major turning point in the rights of the handicapped, meaning that a child could enrol in a secondary school without discrimination in Italy, although since 1977 'handicapped pupils' had been included in primary education.

Integration

The Law of 1977 finished off the process of integration begun in 1971. The law concerned itself with the success of every child, especially the handicapped child; it regarded school class unity as paramount and set aside a maximum of 160 hours per year for separate out-of-class activities. It also provided for the training and use of specialist teachers and the maintenance of a school-support team (socio-psychopaediatric team).

The school-support team (the socio-psychopaediatric service)

This was created to look after the welfare of children in the school system and to deal with any physical or mental problems which the children may have. In the school the team provided much needed support for the teachers whilst outside they liaised with health authorities. All employees of the Service had to be graduates with appropriate degrees and diplomas.

Successive provisions after 1977

The Ministerial Directive in 1979 abolished Latin in the curriculum and made modern languages and technical subjects obligatory in secondary education, as well as seeking further integration in secondary schools. Greater flexibility in the nursery school system was facilitated in 1982, and teachers were trained to deal with particular special needs; but integration was still held to be subordinate to the educational programme.

For many years, because there was no actual law to the contrary, handicapped pupils found it very difficult to go to secondary schools. Later legislation also only provided for integration in nursery and primary schools; secondary schools were largely ignored. Rather, it was important regional legislation which provided the first steps to secondary integration. In particular in Veneto in 1980, in Friuli Venezia Giulia in 1981, in Sicily in 1981, and in Calabria in 1984.

Before the Constitutional Court's ruling in 1987, secondary integration had been considered, but never made obligatory. The ruling demanded integration on the same terms as in primary schools. The testing of disabled candidates was also reviewed and accordingly allowances were made: those who could not write had their answers written down by an examiner; in oral examinations those who could not speak were allowed to write down their answers.

Given the special circumstances of handicapped pupils, the Government also decided to review the law on financial compensation for disabilities, and in 1990 provided economic aid to pupils with special needs in every type of school at every level (apart from nursery schools) until the child reached the age of 18. The amount received depended on the individual's attendance record and exactly what problem he or she was suffering from (assistance was provided as early as 1988 for deaf-mute children who had not yet learned to speak).

The recent support programmes for the integration of children with special needs are feeling the effects of the present school system. In terms of including all children in schools, Italy is among the more advanced countries in Europe; in contrast to other EC countries, however, the school system had to change to accommodate all pupils and to provide a high quality of education. There was a lack of specialist teachers which contrasted with the fact that generally there were too many teachers; there was no means to appraise or recognize their competence with special children or individuals in specific curricular areas.

None the less, the inclusion of all pupils had general public support and well-organized educational support in schools for the policies proposed. A small but significant aspect of the support for change was the fact that promises had been made by teachers unions such as Convegni di Studio Castiglioncello. Professionals in education in Italy are continuing to confront the problems of children with special needs, but a change in the school system, the interweaving of support programmes into the curriculum, and greater professionalism among specialist-support teachers are what the country is in need of improving at the present time. However, there is active criticism of the existing system.

A conference organized by Co-ordinamento dei Genitori Democration (the CGD) Democratic Parents Union in April 1991, called 'The Child', dealt primarily with children with handicaps. At the conference, a resolution was passed to defeat prejudice and form a new vision of the future. Their national director said that although we talk about integration, there was a need to overcome the intransigency of the school system. It was viewed as incredible that in a country with such extensive legislation for the protection of those with special needs, handicapped children were largely marginalized. It was felt that the failure of some educational measures had resulted from the lack of attention given to the 'handicapped' and their needs. The problem of integration had shown up defects in the cultural order of things. It was often confusedly viewed as a direct 'normalization' of the child rather than a way of finding out what made the child uneasy in a 'normal' situation. It was suggested that it was the country's cultural expectations which often crushed a handicapped child. The arrival of 1992 was also a cause for reflection on scholastic integration considering that school systems throughout the European Community are eventually to be standardized.

Concern is expressed in Italy that in many European countries there still exists a tendency to keep 'special schools' for handicapped children. It is felt that this will only lead to further segregation and is considered a backwards step for some countries which, like Italy, had considered the problems of integration as early as 1970.

Although Italy appears to be ahead of its European neighbours in the establishment of the full inclusion of all pupils in schools, the active work of parents unions such as CGD, should not be underestimated as a force for change. They are constantly lobbying their government for improvements in the system for the success of integrational policies in Italy. This illustrates the need to investigate the practice of integration in EC countries. It is not enough to merely accept that certain countries like Italy are showing a lead in their policies. Italy like other counries in the EC, has its share of problems related to the implementation of integrational policies.

CHAPTER 8

Luxembourg

Luxembourg is officially known as the Grand Duchy of Luxembourg, and has a population of approximately 367,000. It is a small country in central Europe and uses three official languages: Luxembourgish, German and French. It operates two parallel education systems, the ordinary and the special school sytem, and it is necessary to distinguish between 'special education' and 'differential education' in the Grand Duchy.

Legislation in 1963 introduced reform of pre-school and primary schooling, creating the establishment of special classes in ordinary schools for pupils who were unable to successfully follow the ordinary curriculum. Pupils from the Luxembourg community must mainly be grouped in regional classes, rather than in special schools. In 1973 the 1963 legislation was succeeded by a law which created institutions and services for differential education. This law stated that each child unable to follow the special or the ordinary school curriculum without support would receive whatever supplementary help was necessary.

The Ministry of Education is responsible for the educational aspect, the Ministry of Public Health for the medical aspect and the Ministry of the Family for the aspects related to the family and differentiated social education. Differentiated education is presently a vast and well-equipped organization in terms of locations and of personnel (see Table 8.1). The 1973 legislation has formed a basis for the establishment of many centres, institutions and services throughout the country:

a) There are specialised public institutions like:
   - The Institute for Visual Impairment
   - The Institute for Motor Impairment
   - The Medical Pedagogic Centre of Monderf
   - The Childrens Autistic and Psychiatric Institute
   - The Integration Centre

Table 8.1 Differential education in Luxembourg

Specialized institutions (7, as set out in a)	↔	Private institutions (4, as set out in a)	↔	Child guidance services (18, as set out in e)
The professional vocational training centres as set out in (c)		The National Ministry of Education		Primary schooling
The regional centres for differential education as set out in (b)		The Speech and Hearing Centre		The National Commission for Medical and Psychological Pedagogy

- The Observation Centre
- The Language Centre for Speech and Hearing (Integration Classes).
b) The 12 public regional centres created by the Government on the basis of the 1989 legislation.
c) The three centres for professional vocational training.

The differences between one centre and another are based on the philosophy of different forms of 'handicap' which is supported by variation in the material, equipment and resources, the number of pupils, and the personnel. Every institution has its own particular profile, for a number of reasons, linked to origins and focus.

d) There are four private institutions subsidized by the state.
e) There are 18 child guidance services spread throughout the country.

These centres are not endowed with multidisciplinary autonomous teams. They function due to the meticulous organization of psychologists' time, which suggests a strain on services.

The 1973 legislation opted for a social conception of integration in view of the status of the adult handicapped person. In Luxembourg, special education and its particular mode of organization is designed as a means of supporting practical apprenticeships. The Ministry of Education in Luxembourg believes that the intellectual potential, both practical and social, of a handicapped child cannot be realized except with special equipment, a particular methodology and a highly individualized programme. However, differentiated education may be the option chosen after the careful analysis of each particular case, so that positive educational development appears possible in the early intervention for each child. A centre for differentiated education is not the only option. Blind or partially sighted children and children with a mild physical handicap are taught in ordinary schools. Many children with speech and language difficulties benefit from peripatetic education and attend normal school as far as possible.

One particular characteristic of the Luxembourg education system is its emphasis on learning the different working languages, which can present problems for integrating children with more serious learning difficulties. Differentiated education does sometimes co-exist in ordinary schools in the form of separate classes where pupils profit from communal activities but also benefit from a well-organized form of special teaching.

If we look at Table 8.2 we can see that most pupils in special centres are educated in speech and hearing centres, closely followed by pupils in centres for visual impairment. There is a very low number recorded (14) in the observation and integration centres. Numbers in most centres have remained stable since 1981/2 except for pupils with visual impairment, whose numbers have more than trebled. We can also find an increase in the numbers of autistic children identified, and a significant increase in numbers in vocational training centres which answer the needs of adolescents and pupils of school-leaving age.

In an attempt to compile statistical returns, the Ministry of Education in Luxembourg warns that literal translation of these numbers masks the difficulties and arbitrariness of making decisions related to mental handicap. In Luxembourg, a commission of experts, the National Medical, Psychological Pedagogy Commission, regulates the admissions and the transfers in the centres and institutes of differentiated education on the basis of detailed reports. There are, however, ongoing debates within the country about the definitions and categorization of pupils.

The organization and financing of education

Pre-school education

(Based on 1963 legislation.) Children aged 4–6 years are admitted to kindergarten. The fees for pre-school education are mainly supported by the local authority or by private organizations. The state participates in two-thirds of the pre-school support. Pre-school is free in the public kindergartens.

Primary schooling

Every child who is 6 years old before 1 September is obliged to attend school for nine consecutive years (1963 legislation, modified by 1979 legislation). Children remain in primary education for six years, when at 12 years of age they leave to attend a secondary or technical school.

The law imposes on local authorities the obligation to provide primary schools and to provide financial assistance.

Table 8.2 Number of pupils in centres

	1981/2	1982/3	1983/4	1984/5	1985/6	1986/7	1987/8	1988/9	1989/90	1990/91
Centre of Speech and Hearing	180	185	161	170	188	188	190	192	192	220
Institute for Visual Impairment	24	47	43	42	74	80	81	81	82	82
Institute for Motor Impairment	34	36	34	37	39	42	41	40	40	40
Medical Pedagogic Centre	19	19	20	18	20	18	17	19	20	21
The Observation Centre	9	11	10	9	5	6	7	7	4	4
The Integration Centre	11	5	7	7	7	7	8	7	7	10
Regional Centres	253	259	250	251	302	297	279	310	226	218
Integrated in classes in Luxembourg city	—	—	8	8	10	11	11	11	10	7
Institute for Autistic Children	—	6	12	12	16	16	17	17	22	24
Centres for further vocational training and private institutes	265	223	224	259	243	257	274	276	382	392
Total	785	791	770	812	904	922	927	960	985	1,018

Source: Ministere de l'Education Nationale, 1991

The State takes charge of two-thirds of the expenses for personnel in state primary schools and the free schools are subsidized for certain activities. Complementary classes are organized on a regional basis. The State provides 60 per cent of the fees for equipment and its installation, and 80 per cent of the running costs of schools. State primary schooling is free.

Secondary schooling

Pupils are required to remain at secondary school until they are 15 years of age. The 7th, 8th and 9th years of study form a cycle of complementary courses, which give pupils access either to other post-primary education or to a certificate of completed complementary studies.

Differential education

Differential education is provided for all children who, for reasons of their mental or sensory characteristics, are not able to receive their instruction in the ordinary school setting.

Organization

Differential education is comprised of:

a) A diagnostic and consultation service known as 'The Child Guidance Service'.
b) Psycho-pedagogic intervention institutions ie, centres, schools and institutes.

The central administration and direction is undertaken by the National Ministry of Education and Youth.

The Child Guidance Service

This service is provided for the counselling and assistance of parents of children with educational or school problems. Central administration of this service is in Luxembourg, with regional out-centres in the fifteen local areas.

There are about ten full-time psychologists who carry out over 5,000 consultancies each year. This is partly detection work. Severe cases are referred to the National Medical Psychological Pedagogic Commission (CMPP-NAT) which eventually decides on the transfer of a child to a specialized institution, with the parents agreement. The psychologists are assisted by child workers, teachers and appropriate specialized personnel and professionals.

Psycho-pedagogic intervention institutes

On the advice of the CMPP-NAT and with the agreement of the parents, a child will be admitted to a specialized institute, eg, the Centre for Speech and Hearing, the Institute for Visual Impairment, the Institute for Motor Impairment or one of the 12 Differential Education Centres created by the local regions and subsidized by the Government. There are also the private institutes, an integrated 'pilot' class in Luxembourg city, and a class for autistic children in one large town.

Finances

The Government, through their budget, must meet the total costs of the state-run centres, the community centres and part of the private sector. The visits of children to the institutes are free, except when residential or boarding accommodation is needed. The fees resulting from this placement are paid either by the parents, the local authority, or the State, depending upon which regulations are in operation. The boarding annex in the 'language' (Speech and Hearing) centre is free.

Luxembourg is a small country with three official languages. The system is still very much a technical, structured child-deficit model which is moving towards concepts and practices of 'integration' in a slow and cautious manner.

CHAPTER 9

The Netherlands

The Netherlands is a small country in the North West of Europe. The population is approximately 14.5 million and the official language is Dutch. There are 12 years of compulsory schooling. In the post-war years from 1945 until 1960 one of principal functions of education was seen to be as part of the economic regeneration. This investment in the skills and knowledge of the emergent population was seen as contributing to the economic boom experienced in the Netherlands from 1960 to 1975.

The first school for handicapped children was set up in 1790 for deaf, dumb and mentally handicapped children. 'Special' schools were not governed by any statutory regulations until the introduction of the Primary Education Act in 1920 and thereafter several decrees governing special education, including the recent Special Education Interim Act of 1985. The Interim Act will remain in force until more definite legislation in 1995; in the mean time evidence is being gathered for the preparation of a new law in 1995. The Interim Act is designed to encourage pupils from special education into ordinary schools. Both public authority and private special schools receive 100 per cent state funding; 26 per cent of all special schools are public, ie, administered by the local authorities, and 74 per cent are privately run (Ministry of Education and Science, 1989).

Ordinary schooling

There are 12 years of compulsory schooling in the Netherlands, from 5–16 years of age; however, 4-year-olds may attend school, free of charge, if they are accepted by the school.

Schools in the Netherlands are designated as public schools (35 per cent) and private schools (60 per cent) which are run by the Protestant and the Roman Catholic churches. There are also a small number of non-denominational private schools. With the Primary Education Act in 1985 came the school workplan which is drawn up by the school staff and approved by the appropriate authority every two years. The plan includes the school's aims, intentions, organization and pupils' curriculum assessment and reports, including outside support and liaison with other institutions and schools, eg, special schools.

In 1987, the Education Support Structure Act made a distinction between general and specialized support in schools. General support structures offered in primary and some special schools are the school counselling services, of which there are 63 which operate at local and regional level. Special schools receive whole-school support whereas primary schools make more use of individual pupil counselling. Den Boer Kees (1990) refers to the current concern in the Netherlands about the introduction of attainment targets with general educational objectives, which appears to be similar to the attainment targets aimed at key stages in the National Curriculum in the UK, ie, pupils are measured against specific educational targets within a period of time. He points out the basic contradiction inherent in the Netherlands educational system of developing the 'broadening of care', ie, improving the quality of educational provision in ordinary schools for pupils with special needs and at the same time emphazing the importance of cognitive development in a system of assessment which may only lead to more children being referred out of ordinary schools because of their failure to reach these pre-determined objectives!

Secondary schooling in the Netherlands begins for pupils at 12 years of age and is divided into two general parallel systems. One is general secondary education and preparation for higher education, the other is vocational education. General secondary education is divided into junior and senior education, one of which is a four-year course of study and the other is a five-year course, both with six examination subjects. Vocational education takes pupils directly from primary or secondary schools. It also incorporates an apprenticeship scheme with practical work placement.

In 1975 the Dutch Ministry of Education made a commitment to changing the system of schooling which affected special education, both in regular education and in special schools. A qualitative change could be brought about by decreasing the number of children referred to special education, and cooperation between regular and special schools would be increased. A committee was subsequently asked by the Minister of Education in 1977 to advise on a future policy. This committee deliberately established the need for regular schools to 'broaden their brief' while at the same time encouraging special schools to become more specialist and multidisciplinary. This led to the development of activities aimed to foster integrational strategies, eg, the establishment of teams to advise regular schools based at educational advisory centres. There was the added support of the LPC (National Pedagogical Study Centres) to develop the professional competence of teachers in support teams. The new emphasis on special needs pupils in regular schools led to special courses for regular school teachers as well as special school teachers in both initial and in-service teacher training (Drapers, 1984).

In the 1970s school class sizes were deliberately decreased in all schools, by the goverment, although there was also a decreasing birthrate which reduced the total number of classes in schools. The fall in the birthrate did not affect special school attendance in any way. In fact there was a continual growth in the general attendance of pupils in all special schools. From this short historical outline the controversial expansion of special education during the past four decades becomes evident.

Special schooling

Special schools are for children with physical or mental handicaps or with social problems, who are not able to benefit from education in ordinary schools. Of the 14.5 million inhabitants of the Netherlands 109,700 pupils between the ages of 4 and 20 receive special education (Ministerie Van Onderwijs en Wetenschappen, 1992). The Netherlands has some 1,000 special schools, and 7.33 per cent of GDP was spent on education in 1987 (OECD, 1990).

There are 14 different kinds of schools in the Netherlands for children with handicaps or social provlems, as shown in Table 9.1. More than 40 per cent of special school pupils are identified as having moderate and severe mental retardation, which is high, but in keeping with some other EC countries, viz, France and Germany. There are almost 2,000 pupils in one school for speech and language problems, which has become an expanding area of special need in the UK also. Overall, the specialized schooling reflected in this table, with 14 different forms of schooling and a high pupil population, indicate the Netherlands' high degree of commitment to special segregated and specific types of schooling suited to pupil needs.

Admission procedures to special schools

Children are normally initially identified as having difficulties by the parents or teachers in schools. A child will then be referred for 'special' education or help. Every special school has a referrals board which consists of the headteacher, a school doctor or a paediatrician, a social worker and

Table 9.1 Special schools in the Netherlands

	No. of pupils	No. of schools (1985)
Blind children	206	5
Visually impaired children	339	5
Deaf children	930	10
Auditorily impaired children	2,272	30
Physically handicapped children	2,573	30
Children with behaviour problems	5,086	67
Sick/delicate children	2,638	33
Children in hospitals	1,137	13
Mentally retarded children	32,834	325
Severely mentally retarded children	7,818	116
Paedological institutes*	987	10
Children with learning & behavioural disabilities	38,191	310
Children with speech & language problems	1,886	1
Multiply handicapped children	2,563	20
Total	99,460	975

* Paedological institutes are institutes which have ties with a Dutch University or which provide educational advice for special schools.

a psychologist or a special education expert. This board may include a specialist in a particular handicap related to a specific special school type. The board will assess the child and advise the school authorities accordingly. Parents' views are taken into account and they are informed of the assessment procedures and results, and have access to the reports on their child. The final decision on admission to a special school rests with the school authorities. If a child is refused admission, parents may request a review of the decision. Children are re-assessed every two years with the objective of possible referral to an ordinary school.

The State lays down regulations governing school hours, holidays, etc. Children under the age of 7 must attend school at least 22 hours per week. Older children must attend at least 25 hours per week over a period of either five or six days. Each child must receive at least two and a half hours but no more than five and a half hours of education each day. Where lessons exceed three and a half hours per day, children must be allowed a break of at least one hour. The school day begins and ends at the same time for all children. Schools must provide education on at least 200, but not more than 240 days per year. School workplans are drawn up by the school staff and reviewed every two years. The plan outlines the aims, content and organization of the education to be provided by a school, including the subject matter to be covered and the methods to be used to assess pupils' progress.

The school workplan is approved by the Education Inspectorate and applies both to primary and special education. In special education, the general plan includes individual plans for pupils and may be modified in consultation with the child's parents.

The legislation lays down the curriculum to be taught in special education as follows:

- The Dutch language
- Mathematics and arithmetic
- Physical exercises
- Sensory coordination
- Geography, history, social structures and religious movements
- Music, art, craft, games and PE
- The promotion of independence
- The promotion of healthy living.

The curriculum may also include English and household skills. Since 1987, ethnic minority children are offered education in their own language and culture. In addition, special secondary schooling teaches two subjects normally included in the secondary school curriculum. The subjects will vary according to the type of special school. Practical work-based training may also be provided, but it must not exceed 100 days per school year for a maximum of three years.

Schools for children with learning and behavioural difficulties and schools for mentally handicapped children

The schools for children with learning and behavioural difficulties are referred to as LOM schools in the Netherlands, and schools for children with mental handicaps are MLK schools. There has been a considerable increase in the numbers of pupils attending both types of school in recent years. At present there are 326 LOM schools with 40,092 pupils (2,355 of whom are of ethnic minority origin) and 332 MLK schools with 32,222 pupils (4,030 of ethnic minority origin). Approximately 60 per cent of LOM pupils transfer to ordinary primary or junior secondary vocational schools.

Staffing

Special schools employ approximately 20,000 staff, including teaching and non-teaching, full-time and part-time staff. Most of the teaching staff have received specialist in-service training in addition to their general teaching qualifications. The Netherlands has two institutes which provide initial and in-service training for special school teachers.

The staff salaries of teachers, therapists, etc, are paid by the State regardless of whether they are employed in public authority or privately run schools. A separate decree sets out the number and categories of staff to which a school is entitled, which depends upon the type of school and the number of pupils. In 1988 the Ministry of Education and Science spent Fl. 15,000 per pupil on special education.

Education in the Netherlands is free for pupils between the ages of 4 and 16. The parents of pupils aged 16 and over are expected to pay a proportion of their tuition fees, which is linked to parental income. For special education there are various grants available from other ministries and local authorities to cover the extra costs incurred for transport to school, rehabilitation, therapy or special technical aid for individual pupils.

More than half of the pupils in special education spend only a short period of their school careers in special schools. Almost three-quarters of all special schools are privately run and at the same time receive full state funding.

In 1985 the Special Education Interim Act and the Primary School Act in combination set out to expand the theme of integration through the focus of ordinary schools catering for a wider range of learning needs and limiting their power to refer pupils out of the regular system. The intention is that a new Act to actively promote the further integration of pupils with special educational needs will be developed and passed in 1995.

The Special Education Interim Act provides peripatetic support for pupils with special educational needs. When a referrals board decides that a pupil no longer needs to attend a special school, the headteacher of the school informs the parents of transferral to the ordinary school. The pupils who are transferred continue to receive teaching advice from the staff of the special school for a maximum of five years. The amount of time that special education teachers give to pupils in ordinary schools is laid down by legislation and varies according to the type of school. In 1987 supervision was provided for 942 primary school and 2,872 secondary school pupils.

A peripatetic or ambulant consultancy (ambulante begeleiding) is being developed as part of the process towards further integration in 1995. This service would apply to:

- any pupil who has been in a special school for one year and is returning to mainstream school;
- pupils who have transferred to mainstream school, who can receive teaching support from the special school for a settling-in period;
- primary pupils for one year and secondary pupils for three years (maximum).

The Interim Act also refers to four other forms of support to encourage integration of pupils with special educational needs into the ordinary school:

- *Peripatetic supervision* – the extra help given by teachers from special schools to pupils in an ordinary school;
- *Split placements* – the arrangement of teaching part of the syllabus for pupils at special secondary schools in junior vocational schools or ordinary secondary schools;
- *Part-time attendance* – the sharing of teaching pupils between the special school and the ordinary primary or secondary school for part of the week, perhaps in preparation for full-attendance at the ordinary or special school;
- *A liaison committee* would be formed to provide links and networking between special and ordinary education to promote further cooperation between the two educational sectors.

Since the early 1970s many projects have shown that hundreds of children with hearing and visual impairment and many children with physical handicaps have been successfully transferred back to mainstream education after about three years of special schooling. This re-integration has been less successful in the Netherlands with pupils from MLK and LOM schools.

Some of the projects initiated by the Dutch government developed in recent years include the following.

1. The *IPB* (Informatiepunt Basisonderwys) project. This national institute is collecting information about innovations in mainstream schools, where extra personnel and funding are granted for one or two years. The project is an active intervention into means of changing school curricula and analysing the outcomes for the pupils involved.

The IPB receives reports from teams of teachers in schools including new curricular materials and observations, eg, in reading methods. A journal is subsequently published which disseminates the results of innovations and interventions in schools to teachers and other professionals.

2. *GEON* (differentiated education) has developed a number of small courses aimed at supporting teachers in developing pupils in autonomous activities. The teachers in the schools are supported by tutors who offer directions about how to teach pupils with special needs in independent learning, and advice is given about organizational factors necessary to stimulate pupils' self-supporting activities.

These are just two examples of the many funded research projects which inform the present situation and which are attempting to reform the didactics and traditional curriculum which underpin the Dutch education system.

Numbers of pupils in special schools are now in excess of 106,000; therefore special education is still expanding. Franke (1991) suggests that regular schools need a form of internal coordination and organizational structure to bring about more success in integration. He implies that classes are too big and not enough time is devoted to pupils with special educational needs in mainstream schools.

Movement and momentum towards strengthening ordinary schools for the support of pupils with special needs involves a number of proposals to the National Assembly; the first of which is the restriction of the growth of special education, and the second is the improvement of support systems in mainstream schools. The measures proposed for restricting growth include:

- The freezing of personnel strength at the level of 1 August 1987.
- The freezing of material facilities at the level at the level of 16 January 1988.
- The suspension of procedures for the establishment of 'new' schools.
- Investigation of the possibility of offering special education to children with learning disabilities under the age of 6, at primary schools.
- The employment of staff personnel beyond 1 August 1987 level for support tasks in mainstream education (both primary and secondary).

There is also a need to improve the support system in mainstream education through the following plans:

- Regional cooperation between mainstream and special education by the formation of advice committees. These committees will consist of experts who will determine whether or not pupils should be referred initially or whether pupils with learning disabilities will be supported in mainstream education. If the committee is of the opinion that support should be given by mainstream education, referral to special education will not be considered. Furthermore, the committee is responsible for indicating the specific support necessary for the individual pupil in mainstream education.
- The committee is obliged to plan a follow-up system for each of the pupils, as well as pedagogical/didactical reports.
- The creation of team-centred projects in mainstream education. Because the recognition and diagnosis of learning problems usually remains restricted to the schools and teachers themselves, it is important to encourage wider dissemination of information about pupils. The wider sharing of responsibilities for pupils' educational needs can be achieved through the formation of teams and the inter-professional development of provision. Behind this policy is the expectation that team-centred processes will develop that will form a follow-up for pupils over a number of years.

- The expansion of professional development is needed to increase expert knowledge. These training courses are particularly intended to make teachers identify and understand their own actions when dealing with pupils with learning problems and to learn how to design educational programmes.
- The cooperation of mainstream primary and secondary special education by way of a number of projects. The general aims are both a reduction of the number of pupil referrals out of ordinary schools and the actual participation in special education.
- The development of partial or part-time participation and eventually the return to mainstream education of pupils from special education, eg, attendance at lessons in practical skills at some secondary schools by pupils from special education. The belief is that through part-time participation, pupils stand a better chance of success when returning to mainstream education.

Integration

One of the Interim Act's main aims is the promotion of integration. Where possible, pupils are encouraged to remain in ordinary schools or to transfer from special to ordinary classes. In the Primary Education Act, 1985 there is provision to facilitate this process by improving the ability of ordinary schools to meet the educational needs of a wide range of pupils.

A policy laid down in the Act caters for the needs of individual children through individualized and differentiated teaching, accounting for differential paces of learning. This policy also applies to pupils who need extra help or support. At present, attention is being focused on reading in the primary curriculum. This situation will be reviewed shortly to establish whether reading should be prioritized within the curriculum or if mathematics should be given the same priority.

Ordinary teachers may have 32 hours of in-service training in preparation for teaching of a wider range of pupils. The courses are voluntary, and may be taken during school hours. They are paid for by the State. Primary schools with large numbers of pupils with special educational needs are entitled to extra teaching staff.

Recently, an integration project has been started to link ordinary schools with special schools to foster pupil integration. This project is referred to as WSNS, which is an abbreviation of the Dutch for 'Going to School Together Again'. There are 226 cooperation centres which are to begin the project in August 1992. These centres are being established to coordinate integration between ordinary and special schools. Regional managers are being appointed to accomplish a network of these centres. The plan is that 15 ordinary schools will link with one special school in an area to form a local cooperation centre. The outcomes of this project have not yet been evaluated.

One is forced to question the steep growth of pupils in special education in the 1970s when we know that educational policy has set out to slow down the growth of special education. The special schools themselves, in terms of offering a special curriculum and in modifying their admission policies according to supply and demand, have been successful in capturing the approval of parents and pupils. It is also suggested that many regular schools have their pedagogic and didactic problems, so parents deliberately choose the special schools as an alternative (Heyning and Kropveld, 1989). However, the evidence from the Netherlands appears to point to a lack of confidence in the ability to support pupils with special educational needs completely within the regular schools.

Rodbard (1990) in his comparison of the educational systems in the Netherlands and the UK, notes the high regard and lack of stigma associated with special schools in the Netherlands. He rates highly an integrated approach to school support systems in the Netherlands because of the close association between support for individuals and groups of pupils, and the support for teachers by a wide variety of professionals. He also commends the use of contracts between schools and support centres as an effective device to establish work patterns and to provide the basis for evaluation and future planning. The Netherlands is unique in the European context for its highly developed and well-supported special school system which is expanding and growing in spite of the counter-efforts to establish 'integration' or mainstreaming as a legitimate form of schooling for pupils with special educational needs.

CHAPTER 10

Portugal

Portugal is a small country in South West Europe. It is officially known as the Portuguese Republic and has a population of approximately 11 million. There are ten years of compulsory schooling and the official language is Portuguese.

General context of special education in Portugal

The organization of a special education system started very late in Portugal, compared to other European countries. In 1960, most handicapped children were still educated in hospitals or were living in private institutions run by charity associations, totally separated from the rest of education. Special classes for 'educationally subnormal children' had been created in Lisbon and some urban centres in 1946, but this initiative represented an isolated measure adopted by the Ministry of Education; the needs of children with marked disabilities were not yet recognized by the government.

Special provision for other categories of handicaps were created later; the first special schools for deaf, blind and mental handicapped children were opened between 1965 and 1976 under the initiative of the Ministry of Health and Social Welfare (Costa, 1981), which also supported the first experiences of integration of blind students in secondary schools. During this period, 30 special schools were provided. These first steps represented an important contribution to the implementation of special education services in Portugal.

A huge task has been faced by special education teachers, parents associations and local services during the process of change the country has passed through after the fall of Salazar's regime in 1974. There were few special schools and they were mainly located in urban centres; many handicapped children living in rural areas did not receive any education. This lack of resources contributed to the search for diversified and flexible forms of provision for the special needs population.

A quick process of democratization created a social and political climate which made integration policy implementation easier within a short period of time. Equality of rights, anti-discrimination and non-segregation had become familiar terms and they concerned not only the handicapped population but other minority groups too. For the first time in 50 years, Portugal had free unions, associations and all sorts of popular initiatives claiming the rights of different groups of people, and for their participation in the creation of new structures and in the search for new solutions to their problems. Schools naturally participated in the whole process of change, both at institutional and educational level.

The social benefits of integration and full access to mainstream had become the major goals of the integration movement in education. But many special schools had opened by that time, as a result of parents associations' initiatives, which became influential as pressure groups claiming the right to education for mentally handicapped and multiply-handicapped children.

During the last 18 years, gradual steps have been taken through the initiative of the central department of Special Education at the Ministry of Education in Lisbon towards the creation of a sub-system of special education which would help the country to recover from its lack of resources and from isolation from the rest of Europe. Strong links had to be created with regular education for a progressive unification of both systems and for the creation of a new school system ready to respond more and more to the needs of all children.

A gradual decentralization process made the creation of regional services of special education possible. Local services to support integration programmes had been created without a strong legal framework, and were absorbed by local education services. The coordination of different forms of provision became easier and it contributed to the gradual establishment of cooperation schemes and better liaison with special schools.

The integration process

Some strategies were adopted to facilitate the integration process and to mediate the necessary adaptations in ordinary schools according to the individual child's needs, from pre-school (0 – 6 years) to secondary level. Portuguese schools had no tradition of remedial teaching services or compensatory education for children with school failure or social problems, who sooner or later were banished, as a general rule, from the regular system.

Additional human resources and the expertise of qualified, experienced teachers were absolutely necessary to support schools and to attain good quality integration programmes. Two main priorities were established from the beginning of the whole process:

1. The development of special education post-graduate teacher training courses (2-year full-time courses).
2. The creation of regional support teams (including teachers, mobility technicians, speech therapists, etc.).

The creation of special education training was important; so too was the progressive development of a broad network of regional support teams which has since taken place all over the country under the initiative of the Ministry of Education (Fernandes, 1989).

General aims and areas of intervention

The first regional special education teams were created in 1976 with the main goal of guaranteeing social, community and school integration of handicapped children in the normal environment. The experience that had been accumulated during the experimental period of implementation with the local services had contributed to their official recognition and consequent definition of their main competences in 1988 (Ministry of Education, 1988).

The lack of coordination between health, social security, education and pre-vocational services had reinforced the need to establish permanent liaison between all community services which became progressively involved in the education process of handicapped children at local level. This situation, and the lack of resources in rural areas, had broadened the competences of special education teachers who had to assume a multidimensional role. Itinerant and peripatetic teachers have become the major 'pivot' of the integration process and the main link between ordinary teachers and the handicapped child's family and social environment.

The contribution of these local teams to the process of screening and referral of handicapped children was extremely useful. Intensive contacts with local hospitals, social services, community associations, local authorities and so on have been developed in order to promote a systematic and efficient liaison between them, and to provide guidance and a comprehensive support system to the handicapped child's family as early as possible. Finding a solution to the parent's health and work problems was sometimes the first step in helping children living in deprived areas.

At the educational level, itinerant pre-school teachers were also in charge of early intervention programmes based on parents' guidance and the child's stimulation (at home, or in playgroups, nurseries, and so on) and of integration programmes at pre-school level.

The lack of infrastructures was and still is a problem. It was and still is important to implement an adequate support system for integration programmes, bearing in mind their continuous improvement and permanent adaptation to the individual child's needs. The concrete problems dictated by everyday practice were felt by practitioners as an imperative to address before their intervention in schools could be successful. The urgency of quick solutions had somehow created a certain 'pioneering' spirit and idealism, with all their dangers, but on the other hand it had the advantage of having become an important element of pressure for the search for creative solutions and better rationalization of available resources at local and national level.

Two concrete examples illustrate the great effort that has been developed to create new services, to support integration programmes and improve their quality.

1. *Special education resource centres* – the first one was created in Lisbon in 1976 by support teachers' initiative, in order to provide Braille books, materials and resources for special needs pupils, which were sent to regional support teams and taken to ordinary schools by itinerant teachers.

2. *Multidisciplinary teams* – were created much later on an experimental basis, but had not yet responded to the wider needs of the country. Assessment and guidance have always been seen as a major area of need in the support of integration programmes and the guarantee of a comprehensive assessment of the special needs population.

The first multidisciplinary teams were also implemented on an informal basis, and they represented an important step for the recent official recognition of their great value in the actual context of reform of the education system (Law no. 319/91). During the experimental phase of implementation of these guidance teams (in five regions of the country), special schools' human resources (psychologists, social workers, therapists, etc.) have cooperated with support teachers in the assessment process and in the coordination of the individual education plan of the special needs population.

Assessment, planning and interpersonal skills training have become a priority for the establishment of effective cooperation links with parents, regular schools and many professionals, with whom the support teachers have to interact on a permanent basis.

Structure and organization

The first regional teams were settled in the main cities of every district of the country. Their rapid expansion has gradually reduced the long distances itinerant teachers had to drive to reach the most distant villages, where no special education services were available.

The composition of these teams may reach the maximum of 25 professionals. They usually meet weekly under the coordination of a teacher, who becomes the main link with regional administrative and education services. Their meetings usually take place in a regular school or in any other place offered by the local authorities for that purpose. All handicapped children from 0–18 years old, living in the same geographical area, are distributed according to their age level among the different members of the local team (many teams have pre-school, primary and secondary school teachers), who immediately contact their families and schools and who support the pupils throughout their school life.

Diversified and flexible forms of provision for children with special needs are increasingly available in Portugal. The choice depends mainly on the nature and severity of the impairment. Itinerant support systems are more adapted for visually and physically impaired children, and special units and resource rooms are the most common form of provision for deaf and mental handicapped pupils.

A significant number of itinerant teachers (521 at national level) shows the important role this form of provision still plays, particularly in rural areas, in the achievement of a complete integration of a handicapped child into his or her own school community. Special transport and other kinds of facilities have progressively become available through the cooperation of the local administrative services whenever appropriate support is only available in the neighbourhood school.

In the recent context of reform of the education system, the organization of support systems to primary and secondary schools tends, nevertheless, to become settled on a permanent basis in many regions. Special education teachers are viewed more and more as additional human resources who must not act as external 'experts' in handicap, but as full members of the teaching staff.

This gradual 'integration' process was an important step in the improvement of cooperation and links between teachers, as well as being a strategy to help ordinary schools to assume their new role and to achieve a better management of children with special needs.

Another significant variable concerned the distribution of special needs pupils to every support teacher, considering the distances between schools, the time spent in travelling and the variety of tasks that had to be accomplished outside the school. According to a recent survey (Correia, 1990) after 1982/3 the number of regional teams increased substantially, from 29 to 109. This 'explosion' represented a new phase of consolidation in the integration policy, but it also reflected the decision to include 'mentally handicapped' and other groups of mild special needs, with mild and moderate learning difficulties pupils into mainstream programmes. The ratio of special needs pupils per support teacher varied greatly according to the pupil's school level, the degree of impairment, available human resources in every region and forms of provision. An estimate of between 1:8 and 1:10 has nevertheless been calculated as the average ratio.

Support to schools

There are multiple professional tasks which are part of a support teacher's job, particularly in rural areas where resources are not sufficient and a great effort must be made to coordinate the information and cooperation of community services. It is important for the gradual liaison between services that the main focus of special education teachers' intervention lies in the school and in a close cooperation with parents and teachers.

The resource specialist acts basically as a consultant to the regular classroom teacher, helping him or her to make adaptations in methods, teaching strategies and content according to the specific needs of the handicapped child. This is particularly the case for pupils with sensory or physical impairments when the expertise of itinerant teachers of the specific learning needs of these pupils becomes absolutely necessary to help ordinary teachers to feel more self-confident. The support teachers are also mainly responsible for the implementation of an education plan which always includes specific areas where the child needs particular training, eg, Braille, mobility and self-help skills.

Close cooperation with the regular teacher inside the classroom is becoming more and more frequent, particularly in schools where the number of children with special needs is larger, and flexible forms of learning support become necessary on a permanent basis. In many primary schools, the support teacher is becoming less and less the expert in visual or physical impairment, but is a useful school resource in curriculum adaptations, assessment procedures, classroom management, new technologies and so on.

Underlying principles in the integration process

Some underlying principles have directed the integration process and the strategies adopted for the progressive normalization of handicapped people into society. They are based on general assumptions which have been adopted at international level, but they assume a particular meaning in a country which has had to find its own way, and which clearly adopted (even with its own contradictions) a policy of integration as the main strategy to solve the problems of the special needs population. These principles can be defined as follows:

1. A principle of normalization which will only be attained by early integration in the natural environment and full participation of handicapped children in their own community life.
2. Sharing the same opportunities and participating in the daily life of the local school as a full member, is the best way of preventing handicapping conditions developing and for achieving a change of attitudes towards children with special needs.
3. Learning together and permanent interaction with peers, through participation in the same curricular activities as other pupils as far as possible, is the most efficient strategy for the training of social skills.
4. The progressive responsibility of the regular school for the special needs population requires the close support of well-trained professionals, who must cooperate with teachers as their partners and share in some of the teaching tasks.
5. Flexibility and adaptation to the individual learning needs of *all children* by the regular system is a long, ongoing process involving deep mechanisms of change in the actual educational and social context, which will only be achieved through successful concrete experiences of the integration of pupils with special needs in normal educational contexts.
6. The organization of special education resources must be totally flexible in order to support all those who are involved in the education of handicapped children as true *partners* – community services, parents and schools.

Two major changes in the educational system which have directly affected the organization of special education in Portugal are:

- the decentralization in education and the creation of four regional education departments to coordinate special education services throughout the country;
- the expansion of an integration policy which is increasing the number of children and young people in ordinary schools, from pre-school to secondary level.

According to a recent statistical survey undertaken by the Ministry of Education, 79 per cent of the school population with special educational needs attend mainstream schools and only 21 per cent attend special schools (DGEBS, 1992). This appears to show a rapid expansion in integrated education, because in 1982/3 there were 60 per cent of these children attending special schools and only 40 per cent were integrated into ordinary schools. Ten years ago, there were only 29 special education teams, consisting of support teachers, psychologists, speech therapists, etc, which attended to 3,323 children. In 1990/91 there were 199 teams with 2,800 teachers looking after the special needs of 27,075 pupils. The total population of pupils with special educational needs being attended to by the special education support teams is shown in Table 10.1. As with other European countries, the biggest group of children are those with learning difficulties (32.4 per cent) closely followed by children with mental handicap (29.1 per cent). Together they make up 61.5 per cent of all special needs pupils receiving help in Portugal. However, if this group is combined with students identified as 'emotionally disturbed', then these three categories make up almost three-quarters of all students with special needs, which is a significantly high number.

The expansion of the integration movement in Portugal is further confirmed by the government's implementation of integration through the deliberate creation of vacancies on certain courses in schools. The number of handicapped pupils admitted under the special education clause, which forms part of the educational policy in Portugal, is:

52 pupils during 1980–90
62 pupils during 1990–91
74 pupils during 1991–92

It appears that numbers of SEN pupils are increasing in school inclusion each year. There was an average of five pupils per year integrated in the

Table 10.1 Pupils being attended to by special education support teams in 1990/91

Pupils	Numbers	%
With hearing impairment	2113	7.8
With visual impairment	1241	4.6
With mental handicap	7910	29.1
With physical handicap	2622	9.8
With learning difficulties	8770	32.4
With emotional disturbance	3472	12.8
With deafness/blindness	58	0.2
With chronic illness	889	3.3
Total	27,075	100

Source: DGEBS, 1992

ten years from 1980 to 1990. Numbers in the last two years are substantially greater, with 136 pupils admitted over a two-year period (Lisboa, 1992).

Future trends

A period of consolidation of all this experience started some years ago, but deep changes in the general system are necessary for a large qualitative step in integration practice. The implementation of the ongoing reform of the education system will be the only guarantee of some deep modifications education must pass through to be able to respond to the needs of all pupils, not only to those with a visible handicap. Integration of special education resources in the mainstream system can become a valuable instrument of gradual improvement of teaching practice and modification of the whole school environment.

A law published in 1991 represents a significant step towards that direction. Deep modifications in school organization, curriculum, evaluation, forms of provision and so on, have been officially recognized as a priority for the guarantee of full access of special needs pupils to the mainstream. Ordinary schools have definitely become the main setting for the education of as many children as possible. Portugal is a country struggling to find the best means to educate and integrate a large number of children into schools, who until recent years had no educational opportunities at all.

CHAPTER 11

Spain

Spain is a large country in the South of Europe, with a population of approximately 39 million. There are 11 years of compulsory schooling and Castilian Spanish is the official working language.

A new model of special education

In recent years, understanding of the possibilities for development, and the delimitation of certain disabilities in life generally, and in schools in particular has spread within the educational community and within Spanish society as a whole, in a dramatically forceful manner.

In the educational community, school life and education practice, and the concept and design of educational services, are being altered by the acceptance of the principle of school integration. There is a re-assessment of the traditional role of special schools. The change centres around the introduction of the concept of 'special educational needs'. In Spain, this concept is linked to certain kinds of pedagogic help or services required to achieve the pupil's educational aims, ie, an educational need is described in terms of what is essential for the achievement of educational objectives. Educational needs are therefore seen to be continuous, requiring action and resources which may be specialized or mundane and will include both temporary and permanent help and services.

The Spanish concept stresses the fact that what must be taken into account is not the categorization of people according to the available resources, but the conditions which affect the personal development of pupils and which justify the provision of particular help or services. This concept also emphasizes the responsibility of the school in optimizing the pupils' development: 'special educational needs of a student must be identified in relation to the school context and it is only from this context that a solution can be found' (Embajada de Espana, 1992).

A student's special educational needs are seen in Spain to be of an interactive nature and are relative to the situation, which implies the inter-action within that context with teachers, peers, the structure and organization, which may be remoulded to find a solution to each student's learning difficulties. There emerges a vision of the school as encouraging the complete development of all students, whatever their individual character-istics. The school is an entity which responds in different ways to human diversity.

The new concept of special education brings with it two functions. One is the search for a situation as least restrictive as possible, and the other is the diversification of what is offered by schools. It is urged that the practice of automatically establishing services according to the nature of the handi-cap should be abandoned and replaced by a concept of resourcing individual needs.

Parents are seen as an integral part of this new development. Their involvement is to be encouraged through the School Council, Parents Committee and on a personal level. Their involvement is seen as crucial from the initial identification of the student's special educational needs to the subsequent action and follow-up. This cooperation is felt to affect educational development other than the merely academic.

Just under 23 per cent of the population of Spain is under the age of 18. In 1987, pupils in special education represented between 1 per cent and 2 per cent of all pupils in education (see Table 11.1). More recently, the percentage has risen to 2.3 per cent of pupils in special schooling (Gortazar, 1991). In Spain, compulsory education now extends to all pupils between the age of 6 and 16 years. Up until the passing of the General Education Law in 1990, pupils left school at 14, and compulsory education comprised three cycles within the eight years. Now, however, bringing the education system into line with other European countries, primary education is ex-tended from 6 to 12 years of age and secondary education from 12 to 16 years of age.

Like some other EC countries, Spain has a high dependence upon private

Table 11.1 Pupils in education

Pre-school	Primary	Secondary and vocational	Higher	Special	Total
1,084,752	5,575,519	2,000,080	960,936	106,106	8,766,457

Source: Ministry of Education and Science, 1989

Table 11.2 Public and private schools, 1988

	Public	Private	Total
Pre-school	279	564	843
Primary	6,651	1,633	8,284
Secondary	613	654	1,267
Vocational	465	428	893
Special education	85	130	215
Total	8,093	3,409	11,502

Source: Ministry of Education and Science, 1989

schooling, especially in the pre-school stage and in special education (see Table 11.2). Many of the private schools receive state funding and are subsequently inspected and advised by Ministry of Education officials.

However, the main focus in the segregated private sector is on schooling for specific disabilities which is rooted in the history of charitable organizations like ONCE (The National Organization for the Blind in Spain), and the general view in the past that people with disabilities and handicap were the responsibility of the social welfare system and religious charities. It was in the 1960s and 1970s that parents' action led to the establishment of special schools in Spain under the aegis of the Ministries of Education and Social Services who together operated support for care and education eg, speech therapists and teachers providing support in schools.

Special schools accomodate the needs of pupils with mild, moderate and severe mental handicap (or learning difficulties). There are schools for pupils with physical disability, and with sight and hearing problems. Pupils with multiple handicap are educated in the school which best meets the predominant needs of the child. The Ministry of Education in Spain has designated 43 ordinary schools for the education of pupils with physical handicap. These schools receive the services of support staff, ie, extra teachers, care assistants, special therapy and physiotherapy.

Table 11.3 shows the figures for pupils in special education centres in 1988/9 according to their major 'deficiency'.

The highest percentage of pupil numbers, ie, 62 per cent are found in the area associated with learning difficulties, both moderate and severe. The pupils with 'emotional' problems form the next largest group, with 7 per cent of all pupils in special centres. Motor and hearing difficulties have similar numbers, with 6.0 per cent and 6.1 per cent respectively. The smallest numbers are associated with pupils with sight difficulties, at just 1.5 per cent. Similarly to other countries in Europe, the highest percentage of pupils are those with 'learning difficulties'. Unlike some other EC countries, there is no reference to ill or sick children or to 'hospital' schooling.

126

Table 11.3 Pupils in special education centres according to type of handicap

Mental		Vision		Hearing		Motor		Autistic		Emotional		Others	
No	%	No	%	No	%	No	%	No	%	No	%	No	%
52,973	62.0	1,300	1.5	5,230	6.1	5,113	6.0	1,716	2.0	5,967	7.0	13,140	15.4

Source: Ministry of Education and Science, 1991

Early intervention

The response to pupils with special educational needs starts in the early years. There is the need for specific intervention and help within infant education and with families. The promotion of collaboration and coordination with other institutions and organizations working in the same area is being promoted. Although early prevention and intervention are seen to be linked to 'health services' in general, the preventative measures which are linked to the early identification of the child's needs and the support of the family are particularly related to educational matters. Therefore, multidisciplinary assessment and adequate family support are seen as essential in the earliest stages.

Equal opportunities for all pupils is the aim of education to be carried out through 'an educational plan', with its foundation in the 'Basic Curriculum Design' which takes into account the identfication and evaluation of special needs and the provision of the necessary assistance and services. The educational plan must call upon the right personnel and material resources, and must provide methodological and organizational changes, both in the classroom and the school as a whole. As far as possible, special measures should only be taken when they are strictly necessary. The Ministry of Education in Spain is continuing the National Plan for integration originally initiated in 1978 for the following five years, directing it mainly to the secondary education sector. For this purpose, special equipment and resources will be considered for significant curricular adaptations with the aim of personal development and preparation for employment. Schools which voluntarily wish to be involved in this project will reduce the number of students per class, employ more teachers and educational resources and will receive preferential treatment from psycho-pedagogic teams. Continuing and vocational education is to be adapted to include handicapped students, with the aim of offering full social integration to all citizens and to increase the quality of life for people with disabilities and handicaps.

Students with special educational needs are assessed through a process carried out by multi-professional teams, cooperating with the school and the family. After the assessment, the necessary pedagogic help is identified for students during the different educational stages of primary, secondary and vocational education; this help is now aimed at each student's possibilities rather than their limitations. Educational and psychological assessment is the basic reference point for taking decisions which affect the curriculum. The subsequent identification of educational needs points to the most appropriate educational action to be taken. It is seen as essential in this assessment procedure that the involvement of all those who are in contact with the child in school, and the parents, is guaranteed.

The White Paper of 1985 focuses on individualized adaptation of the curriculum in accordance with the personal characteristics and abilities of the students. It states that:

Individual curricular adaptation could involve:
a) Giving priority to certain areas of the curriculum, or to certain subjects within the area, when regarding proposals for general school curriculum for everyone.
b) The inclusion of complementary contents and objectives which refer to very specific aspects.
c) Modification of the time allowed for achieving certain curricular objectives.

The modifications suggested for pupils with special needs are promoted as general principles and practices creating a flexible adaptation of the curriculum to meet the needs of all students. The White Paper also specifies that the decision on which type of school a pupil attends is to be taken on the basis of the educational psychological assessment which determines the proposed curriculum, and the subsequent implementation of certain services and assistance. It states that, 'as far as possible, the decision will be made in favour of sending him or her to an ordinary school', and that for all schools, 'flexibility and effectiveness should be characteristics of their organisation'.

Special schools

Special schools are being urged to prevent lower pupil expectations by optimizing the development of personal and material resources at their command. They are asked to adopt unrestrictive organizational systems, both internally and externally within the community, by implementing significant curricular adaptations at all stages within these two principles. Special schools are, however, seen as necessary for helping pupils with the most serious needs, who were previously taught in institutions dependent upon other authorities.

The White Paper stipulates that educational authorities must make a commitment to teachers and other professionals to work out 'a better response' to pupils with special educational needs within the school framework. This will necessitate

- the creation of guidelines, apparatus and models for the identification and valuation of special educational needs and for the diversification of the teaching and learning process, with special consideration for curricular adaptations and organisational models.
- the design of teaching models and materials, and the development of activities in this field.
- the promotion of educational research and the publication and distribution of subsequent materials.

The National Plan for Special Education

The National Plan for Special Education (1978) proposed bringing order to the area of special education, which had been underdeveloped over the years. The plan firstly recognized that the handicapped child had a right to education, a right that had not been previously satisfied. It also recognized that every child should be educated, no matter what the level of his or her needs – an important step that recognized the responsibility of the State in this matter.

The National Plan for Special Education, worked out by a wide group of experts, started off with the following figures on the special needs population up to 18-year-olds:

With schooling – 72,000 (21.5%)
With no schooling – 258,000 (78.5%)

There were 84,000 who needed support or help between the ages of 6 and 14 (figures on schooling of special needs children in 1978, the start of the plan). The plan suggested there was a need to create 77,400 places in specific centres and 180,000 in special classrooms, which would reduce the following year to 30,000 in specific centres and 160,000 in special classrooms (Azua, 1979).

The National Plan was a declaration of new principles which were seen to inspire future planning. It also referred to pupils who presented learning difficulties, and who would make use of the support services of primary education and combined programmes. It made a clear distinction between deficient children and those with learning difficulties and the consequent differentation of the education services between both. There were references to integration at various school levels. When the report referred to schools, it also recognized that the setting-up of special classrooms in ordinary centres would avoid, to a great degree, the widespread creation of specific specialized schools. The schools for special education were intended for those, 'whose education is or needs to be so special that the setting of a classroom is not the place where it can be given'.

The Plan anticipated support at primary level for children with learning difficulties, ie, the training of specialized teachers, who would also act as tutors in the classrooms for special education, supported by a team of assessors. In the special schools, apart from the specialized teachers, other specialist professionals would be called on; among them would be psychologists, speech therapists and physiotherapists.

The principles of the Plan

Certain principles had been established. Among the principles of practice, it was understood that the Plan would respond to a global evaluation of the needs, given that the identification of these needs was one of the main aims of the Plan. It was also understood that the planning of special education would not be based solely on figures, but also on the criteria for quality of the educational response, with sufficient differentiation for all pupils. These were basic principles that were clearly influenced by the Warnock Report in the UK, which specified 'different needs' through the concept of 'special educational needs'.

The basic principles of the right to education, and to an appropriate education, had been established. The understanding was that every person had a right to education, which demanded the maximum development of their abilities depending on the type of disability and their personal level of needs. This point was important as it was the first time that an official document had tried to identify the responsibility of the administration. Education was to be, according to definition, integrated, integral and integratory. The normalization and sectorization of services was to be another principle of the Plan which was to be made clear in two themes: early support and psycho-educational evaluation.

The start of the Plan in practice

The first phase of the plan was reduced to:

- the creation of multi-professional teams;
- the sectorization of services, focused on the localization of Spanish provinces for the provision of resources, differentiating between metropolitan, rural and urban areas;
- the creation of classrooms for special education in public schools.

In the second phase, the sectorization of services was consolidated, creating support teams, multi-professional teams and resource centres. It was intended to carry out integration, starting from the context of special classrooms, and a curriculum of special education was elaborated for specific schools. This process was an important momentum which was put into practice in different ways in the different autonomous regions of Spain.

The Education Law of 1970 established the climate for change. The only new thing was the definition of special education, as an educational form of primary teaching and the idea of creating special classrooms. The complexity of the theme led to the creation of the National Institute of Special Education, which associated itself with the priority of organizing a National Plan for Special Education which finally emerged in 1978. The Plan was an important document, a consensual document, a typical response from the democratic transition, which introduced for the first time terms like integration, normalization and sectorization.

Integration in the Autonomous Communities

In educational matters, the functions of the 17 Autonomies or Autonomous Communities are diverse. In eleven of the Autonomies, education is administered directly by the Ministry of Education. However, the management of schools, staff, inspection and administration of the education system is the responsibility of each Autonomy. The Ministry of Education and Science in Spain (MEC) coordinates government policy at all levels of schooling both private and public. The Ministry also supports and initiates the development of research in education. However, we can find evidence in many of the Ministry's circulars of attempts to encourage and support the inclusion of all pupils in the ordinary school rather than to lay down mandatory requirements for each school.

A Circular, dated 4 September 1981, refers to basic criteria for those who have to govern public and private schooling centres in Catalonia, with reference to special education. In it, special education is defined as 'all those resources of staff, technical and material type provided at different levels of education in the ordinary system so that it fully complies with the constitutional right'. It is not claimed that there is integration, but rather that schools do respond to the educational needs of all their pupils whatever the level of their needs. The circular states: 'We prefer to emphasise the concept of diversity rather than the fact of integration of particular students with disabilities'.

In the Basque country, a plan for special education was developed. The plan pursued two clear goals: the decentralization of services, and the acceptance of 'difference' as an integral part of Euskadi society. Two basic mechanisms or structures were established to carry out the diagnosis, therapy, teaching, professional interchanges and evaluation of the activities developed in special schools and special education classrooms. These were the Multi-professional Support Teams at the schools, and the Coordinating Centres of Special Education in the region.

In Galicia, integration seems to have come up against important obstacles in the early days. The scattered population in rural areas which made planning harder is cited as one of these. In this community, there was a 50 per cent increase in the creation of special education units, parallel to the creation of integration units. Priority was given to 'relative integration', which referred to the creation of special education units in ordinary schools rather than total integration. The plan for special education in Galicia was published in an Order of the Education Council of 9 August 1985. In it, the following criteria for the development of integration were published:

- agreement not to integrate pupils with different educational needs in the same classroom;
- priority to be given to the centres, which include eight primary school units and one nursery;
- when there is a dispersed population, integration to be carried out in two or more schools close to each other which together can undertake the proposed progressive integration.

In Andalucia, a specific plan for the community was not published until 1985. As in the rest of the communities, there had been an important development of multi-professional teams, working together with psycho/teaching teams and teams for early intervention and support for integration. The policy which followed had included the opening of special classrooms in ordinary schools, while providing the schools with extra teachers to help integration. In Andalucia, the integration projects coincided with projects for compensatory education which had allowed for the sharing of responsibility for resources aimed at pupils who had suffered socio-cultural deprivation which put them in a 'high risk' situation.

Integration, it would appear, started in principle with different plans in every Autonomous Community, which will inevitably mean that, after time, integration will have different developments in each of them.

The 1985 White Paper further established the new model of special education in the creation of the two articles dedicated to it:

Article 35.
1. The education system will provide the necessary resources so that pupils with special educational needs, temporarily or permanently, can reach the objectives for them within the general aims of the school system.

2. The identification and evaluation of the special educational needs of pupils will be carried out by integrated teams of professionals with different and appropriate qualifications.
3. Attention given to special needs pupils will be governed by the principles of normalization and school integration.

Article 36.
1. To reach the ends mentioned in the above article, the teaching centres should rely on the appropriate schooling organization, and on teachers of the appropriate specialities and on qualified professionals, just as on the didactic means and materials needed for the pupils' participation in the learning process.

Likewise, they should put into effect the curricular adaptation and diversification needed to facilitate the pupils' attainment of the afore-mentioned ends (Pastor, 1992).

Pastor (1992) expresses scepticism about the extent of the implementation of these principles. She states that if the model of special education mentioned in the White Paper is not widely known, it could be understood that the law contains nothing new, apart from its status as an Education Law. She thinks that it may be accepted as mere rhetoric that Administrations may regulate differently. It is a law that, when referring to integration, compromises a little and ends up not totally in line with the publicly-stated objectives in place since 1985.

The Basque Government had shown a radical move towards integration by this time. A report of the special education committee of the Basque Government showed the momentum towards reforming education for integration. The report formed part of the national movement within Spain and the wider European and international movement towards the inclusion of all students in ordinary schools. The Department of Education of the Basque Country designed a special education plan in 1982 which proposed radical changes in the philosophy and structure of the special education services.

The Basque Plan advocated that the ordinary school should act as the main point of reference in the transformation of education for pupils with special educational needs. As a result of this plan and the efforts of many people involved in education, the following advances have been made:

• Special classrooms have been set up in primary schools.
• Regional Special Education Coordination Centres have been established.
• A new network of local multidisciplinary teams has gradually been developed which now covers the entire Basque community.

- Resource centres for the integration of blind and visually handicapped children have been opened.
- Specific teacher training programmes, as well as initial training and continuing education, have been undertaken for the members of the multidisciplinary teams.
- Class size has been reduced in classes with specific numbers of special needs students.
- Support staff, like classroom assistants and speech therapists, have been provided in ordinary schools.
- Guidelines on school enrolment have been set up to enable parents to obtain the necessary information to help them to find integrative forms of schooling.
- More flexible financing arrangements have been made for special units (Eusko Jawslaritza, 1989).

In the Basque country, a Committee on Special Education was set up in 1987 with the aim of making recommendations on steps to be taken to establish a secure system of development in the furtherance of integration. The Committee consulted with a wide range of people from government departments, parents associations, the Ministry of Education and Science in Madrid, the Autonomous Communities and international institutions. The Committee completed its report at the end of 1988 and have published improvements to be made in the educational system, together with suggested guidelines for putting the improvements into practice.

The significance of the Report lies in the basic principles which underpin the substantial and far-reaching recommendations within the Report. The five basic principles cited are that:

1. The aims of education are the same for all students.
2. A policy of positive discrimination should be used for students with greatest disadvantages and needs.
3. Students' special needs should be seen as relative, temporary, interactive and linked to curricular adjustments.
4. Integration should be an essential part of the educational system, engaging all who are involved in the system, not only the teachers of students with special educational needs.
5. A change of attitudes, aims and practice in schools and in the community must be developed which involves:
   - early intervention from birth – collaboration between parents and teachers;
   - involving the student in taking decisions on educational action;
   - the development of resources within the school system;

- collaboration between schools on provision;
- the coordination of community services such as social and health services to work in parallel with educational services for the best possible support and education of students with special educational needs.

However, on the national level, the Spanish Educational Reform Bill developed the principles of diversity and heterogeneity of students and of education, increased the minimum school leaving age from 14 to 16, and reorganized secondary and technical-vocational education. The National Bill also proposed a series of qualitative curricular reforms which, in association with the principles espoused by the Basque government, are guaranteed to make a great impact on the global education system in the Basque country. The reforms proposed by the Reform Bill dealt with the structures of:

- initial teacher training programmes and professional development;
- innovative curricula, new methodology and technology within the comprehensive school;
- support systems, an increase in the number of support teachers and an increase in help from education teams generally;
- counselling or a continuous process of guidance to involve students, teachers, schools and families to increase and improve the personal and social autonomy of all students.

The recent changes that have taken place in the Spanish educational system and its radical redirection towards meeting the needs of pupils with special needs in a more open, flexible and integrated system, in such a short time, are remarkable. The will, intention and attitudes of the educational establishment in providing the necessary support and procedures for this reformation are also noteworthy. The Integration Plan is ambitious and far-reaching and we must hope that the National Resource Centre for Special Education in its evaluation of this exciting time in Spanish education, leaves us with detailed, documented research into this change process and its effects on the quality of education experienced by the pupils. Marchesi et al. (1991) have already indicated that there has been a successful outcome to the plan for pupils in terms of more positive social adaptations in ordinary schools, more interaction with classmates and good academic results for the pupils in the schools involved.

CHAPTER 12

The United Kingdom

The United Kingdom is situated in two large islands in the North West of Europe: the island of Great Britain and the island of Ireland. It has a population of about 57 million divided unevenly among its four constituent countries (see Table 12.1). English is the official language and there are 12 years of compulsory schooling.

The biggest population is in the South East of England where there are 18 million inhabitants, with 7 million living in Greater London alone. More than 20 million people are under the age of 25, which affects the number of teachers, places in schools and colleges, and the expenditure needed in the education system.

There appears to have been a general fall in the birth rate over recent years and highest school populations are now in the secondary schools rather than in the primary schools. The UK's population grew steadily from the end of

Table 12.1 Population distribution of the constituent countries of the UK

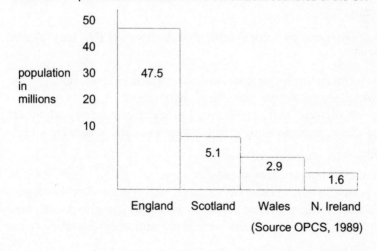

(Source OPCS, 1989)

World War II and included new immigrants from the Carribean and the Indian subcontinent. Since the early 1970s it has remained stable, but the demographic profile of the total population has changed in the 1980s and 1990s. There are more old people now than ever before and there are almost 2 million single-parent families. The great majority of families are small. In over 80 per cent of households in Great Britain with dependent children, there are one or two children.

The school system in the UK

In the UK, compulsory schooling is for children between the ages of 5 and 16; there are 12 years of schooling although, increasingly in recent years, more children begin school at 4 years of age, if they are accepted by the school. It is important to outline the general school system as a large percentage of pupils with SENs receive their education in mainstream or ordinary schools.

Generally, the school system in the UK falls into four levels:

1. Nursery: 3–5 years.
2. Primary: 5–11 years.
3. Secondary: 11–16 /18 years.
4. Further, vocational and higher education 16/18+.

Alongside the ordinary school system there is a similar, parallel special school system for pupils at the three main levels 1, 2 and 3, and often with a combination of 2 or 3 of the levels, eg, special schools for pupils aged 3–18 years.

1. Pre-school

Pre-school provision by a Local Education Authority (LEA) may take the form of:

- *Nursery classes within primary schools* – separate classes for 3–5 year-olds which are an integral part of a primary school.
- *Reception classes* – children who are just under compulsory school age can gain early admission to the first (reception) class in an infant or first school.

Pre-school children may also attend *day nurseries*, which are provided by local authority Social Services Departments, and regulated by the Department of Social Security. Private provision, including *playgroups* and *child-minders*, have to be registered with local authority Social Services

Departments. In 1987, in the UK, some 33,000 children attended local authority day nurseries, 174,000 went to registered child-minders and another 477,000 went to registered playgroups (CSO, 1989).

2. Primary

The legal definition of primary education covers children aged 5–11 years in England, Wales and Northern Ireland, and 5–12 years in Scotland. Primary schools consist mainly of:

- *Infant schools* – for children aged 5–7 years.
- *Junior Schools* – for those aged 7–11 years.
- *Combined junior and infant schools* – these are the most common and cater for children of both age groups.

An alternative system, introduced in some areas in the late 1960s, is the three-tier system, of *lower* (or *first*), *middle* and *upper* schools, based on the idea that the age of 8, 9 or even 10 was a more appropriate time for children to make the transition between the informal integrated teaching of the early years and the more formal vocational and professionally-focused subject teaching offered in the secondary stage. Middle schools developed in a variety of patterns; some catered for 8–12 year-olds, others for 9–13 year-olds and yet others for 10–14 year-olds. Middle schools are confined almost entirely to England; in 1988/9, Scotland had only two middle schools and Wales one (CSO, 1989).

3. Secondary

Secondary education is compulsory up to the age of 16, and pupils can stay on at school for up to three years beyond that.

Grammar, secondary modern and comprehensive schools in England and Wales (and, with different terminology, in Scotland and Northern Ireland) form the secondary school system. Maintained secondary education is now almost entirely comprehensive. The principal characteristics of the schools are as follows:

- *Grammar schools* – provide a mainly academic education for pupils aged 11 to 19 who have been selected on the basis of ability.
- *Secondary modern schools* – provide a general education for those who do not go to grammar schools, usually up to 16 years (though pupils can stay on longer).
- *Comprehensive schools* – accept secondary-age pupils of mixed ability and aptitude.

In Scotland, the closest equivalent to English and Welsh grammar schools were called *senior secondary schools*, while the equivalent of secondary moderns were *junior secondary schools*. (However, the phase 'grammar school' does sometimes appear in the names of particular schools in Scotland.)

In Northern Ireland, a selective system still predominates, though with a few comprehensive schools in certain areas. Corresponding to secondary moderns are *secondary intermediate schools*. About one-eighth of secondary pupils in Northern Ireland attend grammar secondary schools; the remainder attend secondary intermediate schools (Statham *et al.*, 1991).

4. Tertiary

Tertiary education is the third stage of education and is voluntary, non-compulsory post-school education.

Tertiary education is divided into general further education which takes place in colleges of further education, and higher education which takes place in universities, former polytechnics and colleges of higher education. Pupils with special education needs are selected into tertiary education according to college and university admission procedures. There is estimated to be approximately 4 per cent of pupils with special needs in this sector (O'Hanlon, 1992).

Administration

Education in the UK is jointly administered by local authorities and central government, although power is no longer equally balanced between the partners, with local authorities losing and central government gaining. There is variation in the different responsibilities held by central and local authorities in the four constituent parts of the UK, although England and Wales are most similar. Four government departments in each part of the UK administer policy and finances, and at a local level there are administrative areas, or LEAs. LEAs in England, Wales and Scotland are part of local councils which are made up of elected government representatives. In Northern Ireland, Education and Library Boards administer schools in the local areas.

The Department of Education and Science (DES), now known as the Department for Education (DFE) is the central government department responsible for education in England. In Wales, it is the Welsh Office Education Department (WOED) which is responsible, in Scotland, the Scottish Education Department (SED) and in Northern Ireland, the Department of Education Northern Ireland (DENI).

It was the 1944 Education Act which set up a locally administered national educational system. The DES had central control over policy and the LEAs were responsible for most of the day-to-day running of the system. The 1988 Education Reform Act undermined the LEAs' power in two ways:

1. By the establishment of the local management of schools (LMS).
2. By offering schools the opportunity to opt for Grant Maintained Status (GMS).

1. LMS required LEAs to delegate important duties to the governing bodies of all but the smallest schools. Duties include the management of school finances and the appointment (and dismissal) of staff. Funding levels for schools are determined by a standard formula, drawn up by the LEA and approved by the Secretary of State. Funding levels are determined by the number of pupils in schools and must apply equally across all the authority's schools. Recently the proposal is that special schools should undertake their own special form of local management, ie, LMSS (Local Management of Special Schools).

2. The Act also laid down procedures to enable individual schools to opt out of local authority control by acquiring GMS and thus receiving direct funding from the DES; many schools have now successfully applied for GMS.

Special schools

Special schools provide education for children with special needs, on the grounds that they cannot be educated satisfactorily in an ordinary school. They are generally much smaller than mainstream schools: 83 per cent of special schools in the UK have 100 pupils or fewer; 99 per cent have 200 or fewer (1987/8 figures). Special schools often take the full age range, including nursery and post-16. They have a lower pupil:teacher ratio than any other type of school: 6.3:1 in the UK in 1987/8 (Government Statistical Service, 1989).

Special classes and units may also be provided in mainstream schools (especially primary) for children with particular needs, eg, partial hearing or partial sight, 'disruptive' children or pupils with learning difficulties. In England in 1986, the numbers of such units officially recognized by the DES were 1,247 in primary schools and 660 in secondary schools.

The percentages of children with different types of handicap in special schools are shown in Table 12.2 for England in 1982, the last year for which such data were collected.

Since the 1981 Education Act came into force in 1983, children assessed as having special educational needs were given an individual 'statement' of

140

Table 12.2 Categories of handicap of pupils aged 5–15 years attending special schools, England, 1982

	%
Educational subnormal (moderate)	49.5
Educational subnormal (severe)	17.7
Maladjusted	11.7
Physically handicapped	9.1
Delicate	3.0
Deaf	2.2
Speech defect	1.8
Partially sighted	1.4
Epileptic	1.2
Partially hearing	1.1
Blind	0.8
Autistic	0.5
Total	100

Source: Statham *et al.*, 1991

these needs instead of being assessed within a category of handicap. In 1988, 138,000 children in England had statements of special educational needs – 1.9 per cent of the total school population. Table 12.3 shows that the great majority (68 per cent) of children with statements were educated in special schools, and a further 10 per cent were in officially-recognized special classes and units in mainstream schools. About 16 per cent were educated in ordinary classes in mainstream schools.

Since the 1981 Act, the percentage of the UK's total school population educated in special schools has fallen slightly, from just under 1.4 per cent in 1980/1 to just over 1.3 per cent in 1987/8 (Government Statistical Service, 1989). These figures can be further confirmed by reviewing more recent government statistics, given in Tables 12.4 and 12.5.

Table 12.3 Educational provision for children with statements of special educational needs, England, 1988

	%
Special schools (and awaiting admission)	68
Ordinary classes in ordinary school	16
Special classes in ordinary schools	10
Independent schools under local authority	4
Education outside school (including hospital schools)	2
Total	100
Total number of children: 138,067	

Source: DES (1988)

Table 12.4 Special provision in ordinary schools

	1989	1990
Children newly receiving special educational provision under a statement in ordinary schools	10,228	11,084
Children transferring from special schools to special educational provision in ordinary schools	1,159	977

Source: Tables A25/89 and A25/90, DES (1990; 1991a)

Table 12.4 shows that pupils in ordinary mainstream schools are increasingly being statemented as pupils in need of special educational provision. Numbers have risen from approximately 10,000 in 1989 to 11,000 in 1990. There are considerable numbers of children transferring from special to mainstream schools: more than 2,000 pupils in the two-year period. The total number of statemented pupils in ordinary schools has risen by over 20,000 in the last four years, as shown in Table 12.5.

There is definite evidence of an increasing inclusion of pupils with special educational needs in ordinary schools, and further evidence that this trend is affecting the number of pupils in special schools, whose overall numbers have decreased from 7,800 in 1981 to 6,100 pupils in 1990 (Table 1, DES 1991a). Special schools in the same period have decreased from 1,593 to 1,398 (DES, 1991b). Furthermore, the recent Audit Commission Report (1992) indicates that since the passing of the 1981 Education Act there is an increasing proportion of pupils with special needs educated in ordinary rather than in special schools. The Report supported the practice of integration or inclusion of all pupils in its evaluation of ordinary schools, which were said to match special schools in the quality of the learning experienced by pupils with special educational needs. However, it was found that there was great variability in the responses of LEAs to the implementation of the 1981 Act, due to a lack of clarity on what constitutes 'special educational needs' and the responsibilities of the local authorities towards these pupils. There was also a lack of accountability for pupil's progress and school resources, and a general lack of incentive for local authorities to implement the 1981 Act. It was found that the proportion of pupils

Table 12.5 Statemented pupils in ordinary schools

	1987	1988	1989	1990
Total primary, middle and secondary pupils with statements	33,277	40,931	47,262	54,299

Source: Tables A26/87, A26/88. A26/89 and A26/90, DES (1990; 1991a)

statemented in local authorities varied from less than 1 per cent to more than 3 per cent.

The 1981 Education Act

As a result of the recommendations of the Warnock Report in 1978, the 1981 Education Act altered the law relating to the education of children with disabilities or handicaps, henceforth to be known as children with 'special educational needs' (SENs). The Act replaced the previous system of categorization of handicap with the concept of 'special educational needs', which exists when a child has a significantly greater difficulty in learning than the majority of children of the same age, or has a disability that prevents or hinders the child from using ordinary educational resources and facilities. LEAs were given detailed instructions about how to identify the needs of children with a learning difficulty which in the view of the local authority required a specific form of provision for the child. This was written out in the form of a 'statement' of special educational needs and provision; hence we refer to 'statemented' pupils who possess this document, which is a legal entitlement to the special educational provision recommended in the statement. Authorities can design their own individual statements, yet each statement must include:

- the specific authority's view of the special educational needs of the child;
- the special educational provision which the authority thinks appropriate to meet those needs, ie, equipment and resources, staffing and curriculum arrangements;
- the type of school that the authority considers appropriate and, if necessary, the name of the school recommended for the child to attend;
- specific particulars of provision if education is to take place other than at a school;
- any additional non-educational provision to be made available either by education, health or social services authorities;
- all the evidence, advice and information taken into account in making the statement, which must be signed by an officer of the education authority.

The 1981 Act set up a detailed assessment procedure for determining the child's needs, giving parents the right to be consulted about the child's appropriate provision, and to appeal against a decision of the local authority. The Act affirmed, in principle, that children with special educational needs should be educated in ordinary schools as far as possible, if it does not interfere in any way with the education of the other children and makes efficient use of resources. Essentially the new legislation in the UK ensures that:

- Categories of handicap are displaced by new ways of assessing and meeting children's special needs in education.
- Parents are generally encouraged to become more involved in the assessment of their child, and may influence the provision and placement of the child.
- Parents are guaranteed access to information about their child.
- Local authorities and boards must attempt as far as possible, as long as certain conditions are met, to educate children with special educational needs in ordinary schools.

The 1981 Education Act recognizes that up to one in five children may have SENs at some time during their school career. Parallel, though different laws operate in Scotland and Northern Ireland.

Currently, 168,000 pupils in England and Wales – 2.1 per cent of the total school population – have a statement of special educational needs. Only 1.3 per cent of children are educated in special schools.

Since 1983, the implementation of the provisions of the 1981 Act relating to assessment and statements has been reviewed, and further advice has been issued to LEAs, Health Authorities and Social Services Departments on the tightening up of procedures. In recent years, there have been several legal cases challenging the local authority's decision about school placement for individual pupils, the outcomes of which have implications for the procedures for assessments and statements. These cases have led to the revision of certain sections in the guidance offered by the DES. Recently, the Audit Commission (1992) has made strong recommendations on the need to clarify what constitutes a 'special educational need' and the respective responsibilities of schools and LEAs; the need to establish systems to ensure that schools and LEAs are accountable for their work in the area of special needs; and the need to introduce incentives for LEAs to implement the 1981 Act. The Commission specifies that this will imply a new type of statement to increase the focus on educational objectives and accountability through the annual review of pupils and school inspections.

Recent government White Papers indicate that the 1981 Act procedures are under review and that they will shortly be amended to improve the complex and, in some LEAs, slow, process of statementing and meeting the special needs of children.

The Education Reform Act, 1988

The Education Reform Act (ERA) has led to major changes in all schools, most notably the establishment of a 'National Curriculum' in state-sector schools, to apply to all pupils aged 5–16 years. The ERA allows for some exceptions for those pupils unable to follow the full curriculum, as follows:

1. Areas of the National Curriculum requirements may be lifted or modified in specified cases or circumstances, under regulations made by the Secretary of State. For example, where the National Curriculum requires certain kinds of practical work, alternative arrangements might be prescribed in the interests of safe working for those with physical disabilities.

2. Where a pupil with special educational needs is statemented under the 1981 Act, the special educational provision specified in the statement may allow for exclusion from, or modification of, the provisions of the National Curriculum if they are inappropriate for the pupil concerned.

3. Headteachers will be allowed to make temporary exemptions for individual pupils who are not statemented. The Secretary of State is empowered by the Act to make the necessary regulations and these will enable headteachers to decide for an individual pupil that:
   − *either* the National Curriculum shall not apply;
   − *or* the National Curriculum shall apply with specified modifications.
   The exemption or modification will apply for a maximum of six months in the first instance. It is hoped that at the end of that period the pupil might be able to return to an education which fully implements the requirements of the National Curriculum. Alternatively, the period might be used to decide that special educational provision for the pupil will be made under the terms of the 1981 Act.

General provisions

The curriculum for a state-sector school has to satisfy the requirements of the Act which are that the curriculum should be *balanced* and *broadly based*. The basic curriculum is to include:

* provision for religious education;
* the *core subjects* of maths, English and science
* the *foundation subjects* of history, geography, design and technology, music, art, physical education and a modern foreign language (the latter for pupils aged 11-16 years).

Curriculum objectives

The objectives of the school curriculum are that it should be:

* *broad* so that it introduces each pupil to a wide range of concepts,

experiences, knowledge and skills and promotes spiritual, moral, cultural, mental and physical development;

- *balanced* so that each area of the broad curriculum is allowed sufficient time for its contribution to be effective;
- *relevant* so that all subjects contribute to a sound general education which prepares pupils for the opportunities, responsibilities and experiences of adult life;
- *differentiated* so that what is taught, and how it is taught, is matched to and develops individual pupils' abilities and aptitudes.

The curriculum is to further the aims of the Technical and Vocational Education Initiative – making education more practical and relevant to adult and working life and emphasizing personal development, careers guidance and work experience.

The curriculum should also reflect the culturally diverse society to which pupils belong and in which they will grow up. The curriculum should prepare them for all aspects of adulthood – in the home and as a parent; in employment; and in the community and society, locally, nationally and internationally.

The National Curriculum Council (NCC) which is producing the actual curricular documents for schools, reports that it wishes to reaffirm the principle of active participation by the complete range of pupils with SENs (including those with profound and multiple learning difficulties), whether they are in special, primary, middle or secondary schools, with or without statements. It is aware of the very diverse range of special educational needs and does not underestimate the task of achieving participation. The NCC consultation revealed the need for non-statutory guidance on participation and it is responsible for producing detailed guidance and advice for schools which are considering the inclusion of pupils with special educational needs.

The NCC (1989) states:

> …that participation in the National Curriculum by pupils with S.E.N.s is most likely to be achieved by encouraging good practice for all pupils. Special educational needs are not just a reflection of pupils' inherent difficulties or disabilities; they are often related to factors within schools which can prevent or exacerbate some problems. For example, schools that successfully meet the demands of a diverse range of individual needs through agreed policies on teaching and learning approaches are invariably effective in meeting special educational needs. It follows from this pupils with S.E.N. should not be seen as a fixed group; their needs will vary over time and in response to school policies and teaching.

The admission in the document is that schools are not only concerned about the improvement of pupils' learning difficulties, but they may be the cause of the problem in the first place. Good practice in school supports the needs of all pupils, and depends upon the quality of teaching.

It is difficult to define exactly what is occurring in terms of 'integration' in the UK, when provision and services are undergoing major changes as a result of legislation. It does appear, however, that the National Curriculum is viewed as particularly helpful by those who support integration in principle, as it brings more children in special schools up to mainstream standards.

Another factor which has an influence on integration at the present time is LMS. The 1988 Act requires every local authority to prepare a scheme for LMS, under which schemes local authorities have discretion as to whether or not they delegate provision for pupils with statements of SEN in ordinary schools and special units organized as part of ordinary schools. Where such provision is delegated, the formula for allocating resources to schools must take account of the need to meet the particular needs of pupils in such schools. The local authority will retain its duty under the 1981 Act to ensure that the special educational provision specified in the statement is made for pupils with statements and will be expected to reflect this in the conditions of the scheme. It will be for the school to consider how best to deploy its overall resources in order to offer the necessary provision, but it will be obliged to offer what is specified in the statement.

LMS is the delegation of the management of a school to its local managers, which usually consists of the headteacher and the governing body. LMS has been introduced progressively since April 1990 into schools, and has resulted in more schools having a greater say in decisions relating to resource allocation. Schools will need to look at their own priorities for their changing demands on resources, and make their own decisions about what demands financing and development.

In the majority of schools, the most crucial area in decision-making will be that of staffing. The number of staff and the balance of expertise will need to be considered, eg, teaching staff, non-teaching staff and additional staff for children with SENs, with or without statements. There is also the consideration of the financial cost of further in-service training to develop the expertise of existing school staff, which will have to come from school budgets. On top of this, there are books and other materials, equipment, including IT (Information Technology), and library provision, all making demands on the school's financial resources.

There is great concern that LMS poses much more of a threat to the integration process than any previous legislation. There is evidence of increased and increasing demand for segregated provision in many author-ities. The fact that schools can now use open enrolment and that school examination results are to be published will encourage schools to compete with each other academically, which may make them reluctant to enrol pupils with special educational needs.

Local authorities will organize their own budgets and this will offer some protection to statemented pupils, as they are legally ensured of funds. There is evidence of increasing numbers of 'statements' as schools try to ensure money for children who would severely tax their budgets in mainstream education (pupils with SENs requiring extra provision in mainstream). As a result, it will be difficult to implement any new policy of integration now, even where the political will exists.

There is great disparity between local authorities in their use of funding and their support of integration throughout the UK. This is a similar situation to Germany where the Länder are given the same freedom to implement the legislation in a differential fashion. In the UK, we await the passage of time to evaluate the results of the recent upheavals in the education system on the practice and opportunities for pupils with special educational needs.

CHAPTER 13

Local Models for Integration in each Country

School integration projects within the EC framework

The following projects are currently being undertaken by different countries under the auspices of HELIOS, the second Community action programme for disabled people (Helios, 1990). There are a large number of projects in operation in the different EC countries; however, only one example from each country has been included in this book to illustrate the on-going nature of the general committment to integration and the practical means of putting innovatory ideas into action.

Belgium (Flemish community)

LISA (Leuven Integration through System Approach)

This project focuses on work being done in eight groups of 'twinned' state schools, eight in ordinary education and eight in special education.

The main aims of this initiative are: to bridge the gap between the schools of ordinary and special education through the cooperation and functional integration of both systems; to focus on the positive role of special education within this integration process to find the most favourable conditions for the integration of disabled persons in ordinary education; to increase the importance of psycho-medico-social aspects, of the preparation and support given to teachers, and of the direct participation of parents in the deliberation and decision-making process. Five types of initiatives are planned:

- full integration of motor disabled, visually-impaired and hard-of-hearing people at all levels of education, supported by teachers and para-medical staff from special education;

- support for teachers and parents for the integration of moderately mentally handicapped children at pre-school level;
- re-integration within the ordinary primary education system of moderately mentally handicapped children or children with learning difficulties, either after a year in special education or before the age of 13 in ordinary secondary education;
- partial integration of moderately mentally handicapped pupils into secondary vocational education through cooperation between two schools situated in neighbouring buildings;
- preparation of sensory disabled people for the transitory period leading to further education; application of new technology.

Belgium (French community)

Three kinds of work are planned: a critical analysis and evaluation of experiments in educational integration in the areas of sensory, mental and physical disability and learning difficulties; the establishment of working links between ordinary and special schools; and the analysis of barriers to change, both at individual and institutional level and how they function. From this, three kinds of initiatives have been set up:

- a public-awareness campaign for parents, and a training programme for professionals, teachers and staff in both ordinary and special schools;
- the establishment of working links between ordinary and special education;
- the development and evaluation of experiments in educational integration, either in the form of 'special' class integration within an ordinary school or individual integration.

Denmark

The School for Everybody, the Society for Everybody (Hadsten, Hinnerup and Rosenholm)

These local authorities have been running an Educational League since 1976, which works through an Educational Psychological Council for all categories of disabled children aged 0 to 18 years in these three towns (above). The main aims of the League are:

- primary and secondary schools becoming a 'School for Everyone', where disabled children can be educated. School integration must be total, which is why classes attended by disabled children should have only a limited number of places and the support of an additional teacher;
- the Educational Psychological Council should be responsible for:
  - special educational support for children,
  - establishment of vocational training courses for the teaching staff,
  - psycho-pedagogical research.
  The Council changes according to needs, its statute and tasks;
- development of a school curriculum;
- active involvement of parents;
- establishment of social activities for children in collaboration with all services and parents;
- action to increase awareness and to disseminate information at regional level, through the radio, press, public meetings, etc.

France

Educational Integration of Sensory Disabled Children or Children with Psychiatric Problems (Suresnes)

The main aim of this initiative is the educational integration of sensory disabled children (partially sighted, blind, hard-of-hearing, deaf) and children who suffer from psychiatric problems. The areas concerned in this initiative are as follows:

1. Greater Paris: Baguer, Institute for Deaf Children; kindgergartens and primary schools; colleges; and grammar schools.

2. Northern area: EREA of Loos-les-Lille, for children who are blind or partially sighted. Integration networks have been developed in the schools and colleges with specialized structures, fitted with specific equipment and involving the relevant medical staff.

The role of the specialized centre is to provide technical support and to act as a resource centre for teachers who take disabled children. The use of new technology is very important.

3. South-western area: Toulouse, for children who suffer from psychiatric and behavioural problems. The choice of teaching and the developed structures relate to specific needs. For this reason, there are individual teaching projects for each integrated child, teaching projects for the class and the mainstream school; classes linked to a day hospital or rehabilitation centre which take place in a mainstream school; and common projects which link children from special schools with children in mainstream education.

These situations are adapted to the environment and to the initiatives of the different partners.

4. Lyon area: for children suffering from psychiatric problems. The integration of children who suffer from psychiatric problems can be divided into three areas: a care element predominantly for individuals or groups, combined with an educational element provided in specialized classrooms within the mainstream schools. The pupils are integrated in classes for different activities. The most recent element is family guidance, given by the teachers and medical staff. The link between these three elements is provided by regular meetings.

Germany

The Common Education of Disabled and Non-Disabled Children in Primary and Secondary Education (Bonn)

The initiatives in the city of Bonn must be seen against the background of the general situation in Germany: disabled children, who cannot be provided for in the mainstream school, have to attend special school, without the possibility of an alternative choice for parents.

The special schools are mostly of a good standard, the result of very intensive development in the last 20–30 years. In Germany, looking for alternative education for disabled children means finding a way around the established special school system. This is only possible in official experiments with the licence of the Minister for Education.

Bonn started its initiatives for children with all types of handicaps in 1981 – actually the beginning of integration activities in Germany. The earliest experiments in Bonn allowed parents to send their disabled and non-disabled children to an identified primary school class, after which they proceeded to an integrated class in a comprehensive school.

Since 1981 Bonn had been showing initiatives in integrated education. The attendance of children with special needs at the local neighbourhood school was a new concept in education in Germany at that time. Further initiatives were taken in 1986 when nine primary schools in Bonn included pupils with special needs. In 1990 the initiatives have progressed into all kinds of secondary schools, based on parental choice. Pupils with special needs are now progressing through the system of mainstream education in Bonn, which has led integration initiatives in Germany.

The teaching is characterized by all kinds of individualised teaching methods. A lot of – mostly self-made – special learning materials is a good help. Special teachers transfer special education to the mainstream school, but the working time as adviser and teacher is limited in the project.

Greece

Local Model Initiative of Attica (Attikis)

This initiative works with a total of 24 primary and secondary schools in the suburbs of Athens. These are basically ordinary and state schools, and a very limited number of them are special and privately owned.

In ordinary primary schools, disabled children attend special classes for two hours per week and spend the rest of the time in ordinary classes. These special classes are the responsibility of specialized teachers. The extra-curricular activities are organized both at primary level and at secondary level between ordinary and special schools.

The local university uses the initiative for the training of teachers. Other participants are parent associations and pupil committees at secondary school level. Important aspects for work and thinking relate to the organization of both systems: ordinary and special, research into links between the two, the vocational qualification of teachers and the increase in educational integration.

Collaboration is being developed between the educational, health and social services.

Ireland

Experience in Ireland of Educational Integration

The activity groups are organizing 11 local initiatives in Dublin, Cork, Naas and Limerick. State mainstream schools and special schools at secondary and primary level are participating in this activity.

The different forms of integration, as well as the methods used, are wide-ranging, involving full integration of pupils with sensory disabilities at secondary school level, with specialized teachers to give them the necessary support. The schools are making the necessary physical adaptations.

There is full integration of physically disabled people at secondary school level, with the supplementary help of a support teacher as well as medical staff. There is partial integration of mentally handicapped people at primary school level. The children are in a special class but in regular contact with the other children for extra-curricular activities. The common work is increasing for non-fundamental activities. New technology is of great importance in the teaching of these children.

Special classes also exist in some schools where children attend on their own or in a group, working with the support teacher for a short period during the day. The work aims to reinforce the aspects which have been most lacking in their training. There is research into the use of new technology for the education and rehabilitation of disabled children, particularly in the area of communication. Seminars are organized each year for teachers from those mainstream schools where disabled children are already integrated. A specialized centre for physically and multi-handicapped children is being used as a resource centre.

Italy

The Didactic Centre as a Basis for School and Educational Integration (Sardinia)

The Sardinia project has four teaching centres which cover almost the whole island. They are in Cagliari, Oristano, Macomer and Porto Torres. Educational integration takes into account the different socio-economic realities within the regions – the advantaged urban areas and the peripheral urban or isolated rural areas.

The work is carried out with state schools at elementary and primary school level. All the schools follow the same model for full-time educational integration. Twenty-five children are the maximum per class; the teaching work is undertaken by the class teachers and by specialized teachers (for the non-fundamental subjects such as foreign languages, etc.) and reinforced by specialized support teachers. The educational activity of disabled children takes into account the maturity and learning capabilities of each child.

Other services participate actively in the integration of children: they are the USL (Local Health Unit, responsible to the Ministry of Public Health) and AIAS (Italian Association for support to Spastics, a private organization). Both of those services provide therapeutic support either at the school or outside school time, but always in close collaboration with the educational team.

Luxembourg

The Luxembourg project is taking place within the framework of the national institute for visually-handicapped people, responsible to the

Ministry of Education and Youth. This institute aims to assist blind or partially sighted people of all ages in early pre-school, school and further education in vocational training and in professional and social integration.

Since the early 1980s this institute has been developing integration strategies, both educational and social, for visually-impaired people. The specialized staff of the ambulance assistance service of the institute go to the schools, where the partially sighted and blind people are integrated and educated. Furthermore, the institute is acting as a creative design centre which also coordinates the use of equipment and special aids intended for visually impaired people.

The project is currently aiming to help all those blind people attending the different schools and colleges in the capital to become as independent as possible, including reducing their reliance on Braille. The aim of the institute is to teach these children how to use new technology and to allow them to have direct access to school books available in computerized form.

The Netherlands

Education as a Means for Social Integration (Rotterdam)

The main aim of this activity is to improve the situation of young disabled people in the job market by providing adequate training. The main objectives are:

- to stop placing children in special schools by setting up a specialized support system in ordinary education;
- to place disabled children in special schools for the shortest possible periods of time;
- to re-admit disabled school children coming from special education into the normal school system, with the help of specialized and peripatetic school teachers.

The means to achieve these goals are:

- to improve the quality of ordinary education by the introduction of systematic supervision of children and of a 'common consultation' between ordinary and special schools;
- to reduce the number of children in special education through the introduction of a common 'advisory system' between special and ordinary education;
- to introduce a 'movable' help system in ordinary education from special education.

155

Portugal

Use of New Technology in the Education of Children who are
Hard-of-hearing and Motor Disabled with Neurological Problems (Lisbon)

This activity works specifically on the use of computers and on the development of specific programmes for deaf children (100 children, from 3 to 14 years old) and sensory disabled children (150 children from 2 to 18 years old). The aims are:

- to use the computer and related means of communication to develop the social and educational integration of disabled children. Educational integration is carried out in two ways. The first is integration from the specialized centre, which is a resource centre for the child and for the mainstream school. The second one is called 'nucleo de apoio' where the mainstream school has a specialized annexe for children who are hard-of-hearing and share their school-time between the main buildings and the annexe;
- to develop and to improve the capacities of the voice and the intelligibility of the words of children who are hard-of-hearing in their communication with hearing people; children will be able to 'see' their own voice and control its characteristics;
- to develop computer programs on morphology and syntax;
- to develop the spoken and written communication of children with cerebral palsy by using the computer and to adapt the Bliss system on the computer. The use of electronic computer games for children with cerebral palsy, from 2 to 5 years old, is being investigated.

Twenty-five children is the maximum number for a class, and 20 when disabled children are integrated.

Spain

Educational Integrational Project (Valladolid)

The aim of this project is the application of 'normalization' within the educational field, ie, integration in school. This involves combining the ordinary and special school systems, whilst guaranteeing all pupils the service they may need. The work plan of the project is concentrated on the following four aspects:

- organization of existing resources in the field of education, including the reorganization of the functions of special centres as well as the creation

156

of a resource centre for integration work with the children and teenagers with problems;
- development of an educational integration process. This will involve heightening awareness; increasing the number of schools (currently 13) where integration take place; fostering links between ordinary and special centres; and improving teaching and working conditions within the classroom;
- coordination of institutions which care for disabled people in order to achieve a common plan;
- training of teachers both during their studies, and on a continuous basis.

A real emphasis is put on early caring. This activity focuses especially on state schools, but also on private schools. All school levels are included, as well as different disabilities.

United Kingdom

This local model activity focuses on a mainstream first school (220 children aged 4 to 9) in Northumberland, which has taken over full responsibility from a special school for 25 children. This integration project was made easier because, since 1985, the younger children from the special school, which caters for children with severe learning difficulties, have used an annexe on the same site as the ordinary first school. Various shared educational activities had taken place between the two schools and, in 1988, the physical and administrative changes were made. This was the culmination of three years' work involving planning, consultation and discussion with staff, parents, governors, local authority officers and local politicians.

The children with special needs all have significant learning difficulties, but there is a range and variety of abilities and potential among the children. Some are able to walk and speak well; others have difficulties with speech and communication or physical disabilities. Some of the children are profoundly handicapped. All the children follow the National Curriculum as prescribed by law, but children with special needs will work at their own pace on individually-designed programmes which will emphasize social and physical competence, independence and communication skills, and provide as great a range of physical and environmental experience as possible. In the mainstream school, children with special needs have their own class bases but will join other classes for certain curriculum activities if they can benefit from these. A 'tutorial' system enables special needs and mainstream children to work together on a paired basis.

Following evaluation of the successful integration at the ordinary first school, the Local Education Authority is coordinating the next phase of the project which will integrate the remaining 55 children from the special school, aged 9 to 18, with a middle school and high school: these two mainstream schools share a common campus and alterations to the physical fabric began in 1990 to accomodate the children with special needs. In preparation for this merger, pupils and teachers from the special school and the mainstream school are participating in many joint activities. It is expected that, once the arrangements for the full integration of the remaining children are complete, the special school will close completely in the early 1990s.

References

Advisory Centre for Education (1981) *Summary of Warnock Report*, London: ACE.

Ainscow, M. and Tweddle, D. (1992) *Encouraging Classroom Success*, London: David Fulton.

An Roinn Oideachais (1989) *Guidelines on Remedial Education*, Dublin: Department of Education.

An Roinn Oideachais (1992) *Statistics* 1990/91, Dublin:Department of Education.

Audit Commission (1992) *Getting in on the Act: Provision for Pupils with Special Educational Needs: The National Picture, HMI/DES*, London: HMSO.

Azua, P. (1979) *El Marco legal Cuadernos de Pedagogia*, 55–6, pp. 24–5.

Bennett, N. and Cass, A. (1989) *From Special to Ordinary Schools*, London: Cassell.

Booth, T. (1983) 'Integrating special education', in Booth A., and Potts, P. (1983) op cit.

Booth, T. (1991) 'Integration, disability and commitment, a response to M Soder', *European Journal of Special Needs Education*, **6**, 1, pp. 17–24.

Booth, A. and Potts, P. (1983) *Integrating Special Education*, Oxford: Basil Blackwell.

Booth, A. and Swann, W. (eds) (1987) *Inculding Pupils with Disabilities, Curricula for all*, Milton Keynes: Open University Press.

Bovair, K., Carpenter, B. and Upton, G. (eds) (1992) *Special Curricula Needs*, London: David Fulton/NASEN.

BW (1991a) *Bildung und Wissenschaft*, 3/4, Inter Nationes, Bonn.

BW (1991b) *Bildung und Wissenschaft*, 7/8, pp.17, Inter Nationes, Bonn.

Conserjeria de Education (1991) *Special Educational Needs*, London: Embajada de Espana en Londres.

Cope, C. and Anderson, E. (1977) *Special Units in Ordinary Schools*, London: University of London Institute and NFER.

Correia M.L. (1990) 'Educação especial en Portugal', *Educação Especial e Reabilitação*, **1**, 4, p.60–66.

Costa, B. A. – M. (1981) 'Educação especial', in *Sistema de Ensino en Portugal*, Lisboa: Fundação Calouste Gulbenkian, p. 307–54.

Council of the European Communities (1987) *Press release* 1160th meeting of the Council and the Ministry for Education, Brussels.

Cuomo, N. (1991) 'Special Education for the Handicapped and Disabled', paper delivered at Special Needs Congress, University of Malaga.

Daunt, P. (1991) *Meeting Disability: A European Response*, London: Cassell.

Den Boer Kees (1990) 'Special education in the Netherlands', *European Journal of Special Needs Education*, **5**, 2, pp. 136–49.

Dens, A. (1986) 'Belgian contribution to the report on the integration of handicapped children in ordinary schools', in *Progress with Regard to the implementation of the Policy of Integrating Handicapped Children into Ordinary Schools*, pp. 6–26, Brussels, Commission of the European Communities.

Dens, A. (1988) 'Progress report on the integration of young people with special needs in education in the Dutch language area of Belgium', in Kropveld, P. and Diniz F. (eds), *Integration Revisited*, report of the ATEE Conference: Integration of Young People with Special Needs in Education, Athens, 5–11 November 1988.

Dens, A. (1991) The LMA Leuven (short report), *European Journal of Special Needs Education*, **6**, 1, pp. 71–5.

Dens, A. (1992) 'Integration of Disabled Pupils in the Regular School System in the Dutch Speaking Community in Belgium', *The European Journal of Teacher Education*, **14**, 2, pp. 107-17.

Dens, A. and Meskens, V. (1987) *Het Geintegreerd Onderwijs Integrated Education, an analysis of findings on the school year 1985-1986, transmitted by the PMS guidance centres*, a survey made on the request of the Minister of Education (N), Louvain. PMS-Centre for Special Education.

Dens, A., Berte, J.M. and Buyze, E. (1986) *Het Geintegreerd Onderwijs. Een inhoudelijke doorlichting op grond van gegevens van de Vrijs*, Brussels: PMS-Centra.

Department of Education (1971) *Curaclam na Bunscoile*, Dublin: Government Stationery Office.

Department of Education (1988) *Special Education in Ireland*, Dublin: Government Stationery Office.

Department of Education (1989) *The Education System in Ireland: Report by the Department of Education*, Dublin: Government Stationery Office.

Department of Education (1990) *Report of the Primary Education Review Body*, Dublin: Government Stationery Office.

Department of Health (1965) *Report: Commisssion of Inquiry on Mental Handicap*, Dublin: Government Stationery Office

DES (1988) *Statistics of Education. Schools*, London: DES.

DES (1990) *Statistics of Education. Schools*, London: DES.

DES (1991a) *Statistics of Education. Schools*, London: DES.

DES (1991b) *Statistics Bulletin 9/91*, London: DES.

160

DFE (1992) *Diversity and Choice – A New Framework for Schools*, London: HMSO.

DFE (1992) *Special Educational Needs – Access to the System.* a consultation paper. London. DFE.

DGEBS (1992) *Educacao Especial. Dados Estatisticos 1990/91*, Lisbon: Special Education Departament.

Diniz,F. (1989) 'In search of a new approach?', in Struiksma, C. and Meijer, F. (eds) *Integration at Work. The First European Community Conference on Handicap and Education*, pp. 71–83, Rotterdam. Pedologisch Instituut.

Diniz, F. (1991) 'Guest Editorial', *European Journal of Teacher Education*, **6**, 2, pp. 87-100.

Drapers, J. (1984) 'Dutch initiatives regarding broadening the brief, in Conference Report, Implications for Teacher Education of the International Movement towards Integration, Chester College.

DGEBS (1992) The legal basis of special education in Portugal, Personal communication, Lisbon: Special Education Department.

EASE (1990) 'From country to country. Some data about integration in Italy, *EASE*, **11**, 2.

EC (1989) *The European Community Budget*, Brussels: Commission of the European Communities 11/89.

EC (1990) *European Unification: The Origins and Growth of the European Community'*, periodical 1/1990 by Klaus-Dieter Borchardt, Brussels: Office for Official Publications of the European Communities.

Embajada de Espana (1992) Personal communication, Consejeria de Educacion, London.

Eusko Jawslaritza (1989) *Comprehensive and Integrative Schooling*, Bilbao: the Basque Government.

Federal Ministry of Education and Science (1992) *Numerical Barometers: Some educational statistics 1991/92*, Bonn: author.

Fernandes, M. T. (1989) Legal basis of special education in Portugal. Paper presented at ATEE Special Needs WG7 Conference, Athens.

Fish, J. (1991) *What is Special Education?*, Buckingham: Open University Press.

Franke, R. (1991) 'Internal Co-ordination of Provision: A Condition of effective Mainstreaming' paper presented at Conference entitled 'Managing Integration in Europe', Utrecht.

Galloway, D.H. and Goodwin, C. (1979) *Educating Slow Learning and Maladjusted Children: Integration or Segregation*, Harlow: Longman.

Gortazar, A. (1991) 'Special education in Spain', *European Journal of Special Needs Education*, **6**, 1, pp.56–70.

Government Statistical Service (1989) *Educational Statistics for the United Kingdom 1989*, London: HMSO.

Hansen, J. (1989) 'Handicapped Students in the Danish Educational System'. Copenhagen: Ministry of Education.

Hegarty, S. (1991) 'Towards an Agenda for Research in Special Education', *European Journal of Special Needs Education*, **6**, 2, pp. 87–100.

Hegarty, S., Pocklington, K. and Lucas, B. (1981) *Educating Pupils with Special Educational Needs in the Ordinary School*, Windsor: NFER-Nelson.

HELIOS (1990) *Brief Description of Local Model Activities of the Network for Integration in Schools*, Ref H21/VS/CO, Brussels: HELIOS.

Heyning, H. and Kropveld, P. (1989) 'Limiting the Explosion', paper delivered at conference entitled 'Integration Revisited', ATEE W.G.7, Athens

Hodgson, A., Clunies-Ross, L. and Hegarty, S. (1984) *Learning Together: Teaching Pupils with Special Educational Needs in the Ordinary School*, Windsor: NFER –Nelson.

Kirk, S. A. and Gallagher, J.J. (1979) *Educating Exceptional Children*, Boston MA: Houghton Mifflin.

Lewis, A. (1990) 'Six and seven year old 'normal' children talk to peers with severe learning difficulties', *European Journal of Special Needs Education*, **5**, 1, pp. 13–24.

Lindsay, G. and Clough, P. (1991) *Integration and the Support Service. Changing Roles in Special Education*, Windsor: NFER–Nelson.

Lisboa, E. (1992) Personal communication, Portuguese Embassy, London.

McGee, P. (1990) 'Special Education in Ireland', *European Journal of Special Needs Education*, **5**, 1. pp. 48–63.

McGee , P. (1992) 'Ireland: Special Education Under Review', *EASE*, **15**, 2, p. 19.

Madden, N.A. and Slavin, R. (1983) 'Mainstreaming students with mild handicaps: academic and social outcomes', *Review of Educational Research*, **53**, 519–16.

Marchesi, A., Echelta, G., Martin, E., Bavio, M. and Galan, M. (1991) 'Assessment of the integration project in Spain', *European Journal of Special Needs Education*, **6**, 3, pp. 185–99.

Ministere de l'Education Nationale (Luxembourg) (1991), *Education: Enseignement et culture*, Luxembourg: author.

Ministere de l'Education Nationale (Paris) (1991) *L'Education Nationale en chiffres 1990-1991*, Vanves: Direction de l'Evaluation et de la Prospective (DEP).

Ministere de l'Education Nationale (Paris) (1992) *Les Enseignements adaptes et specialises en 1990-1991*, Paris: Directeur de la publication.

Ministry of Education (Denmark) (1989) *Handicapped Students in the Danish Education System*, Copenhagen: Department of Special Education.

Ministry of Education (Portugal) (1988) *Despacho no. 36*, Lisbon: Dirreccao Geral dos Ensin os Basico e Secondario.

Ministry of Education and Science (Spain) (1989), *Estadistica de la Ensemanza en Espana 1986-1987*, Madrid: Centro de Publicaciones de Ministerio de Educacion y Ciencia. Madrid.

Ministry of Education and Science (Spain) (1991) *Estadistica 1988–1989*, Madrid.

Ministry of Education and Science (The Netherlands) (1989), *Special Education in the Netherlands*, Zoetermeor: author.

Ministerie Van Onderwijs (1988) *Educational Developments in Belgium: 1986-1988*, Brussels: International Conference on Education.

Ministerie Van Onderwijs en Wetenschappen (1992) Personal communication from J. Ormel, Zoetermeer.

162

National Curriculum Council (NCC) (1989) *Circular Number 5*, York: NCC.

Nicodemos, S. (1992) *Bulletin of Information in Special Education: School and Social Integration*, Ministry of National Education and Religion. Department of Special Education.

OECD (1981) *The Education of the Handicapped Adolescent– Integration in the School*, Paris: OECD.

OECD (1990) *Economic Survey of OECD Countries*, Paris: OECD.

O'Hanlon, C. (1992) 'An overview of influences and changes for post-16 students with special educational needs', *Support for Learning*, 7, 2, pp. 67–74.

OPCS (1989) *Population Trends*, No. 58, London: HMSO.

G^a Pastor, C. (1992) *Una Escuela Camun para Ninos Diferentes*, Barcelona: PPU.

Pijl, S. and Meijer, C. (1991) 'Does integration count for much? An analysis of the practices of integration in eight countries in Europe', *Journal of Special Needs Education*, **6**, 2, pp. 100–111.

Preston, J. (1991) *EC Education Training and Research Programmes. An Action Guide*, London: Kogan Page.

Randoll, D. (1992) 'The Education of Children with Special Needs in School', paper for Network 14 meeting, Milan.

Rodbard, G. (1990) 'Going Dutch! A perspective on the Dutch system of special education', *European Journal of Special Needs Education*, **5**, 3, pp.221–30.

Schule Statistik (1991) *Die Sonderschulen in der bundeseinheitlichen Schulstatistik 1980 bis 1990*, Bonn: Bearbeitet im Sekretariat der Kultusministerkonferenz, Bonn.

Soder, M. (1991) 'Theory, ideology and research: A response to Tony Booth', *European Journal of Special Needs Education*, **6**, 1, pp. 17–24.

Snowdon Working Party Report (1976) *Integrating the Disabled*, London: The National Fund for Research into Crippling Diseases.

Somers, F. (ed.) (1991) *European Economics. A Comparative Study*, London: Pitman Publishing.

Statham, J. and Mackinnon, D. with Cathcart, M. and Hales, M. (1991) *The Education Fact File*, London: Hodder & Stoughton in association with the Open University.

Swann, W. (ed.) (1981) *The Practice of Special Education*, Oxford: Blackwell.

Swann, W. (1991) *Variations between LEAs in Levels of Segregation in Special Schools 1982-1990*, London: Centre for Studies in Integration in Education.

UNESCO (1988) *Review of the Present Situation of Special Education*, Paris: UNESCO.

Walton, W. T., Emanuelsson, I. and Rosenquist, J. (1990) 'Normalisation and integration of handicapped students into the regular education system: contrasts between Sweden and the United States of America', *European Journal of Special Needs Education*, **5**, 2, pp. 111–26.

INDEX